# THE STORIES WE WRITE

## Collections From Living

# THE STORIES WE WRITE

## Collections From Living

### BY

## CAROLYN FLINN MCCOOL

# DEDICATION

DEDICATED TO ALL the kind souls who identified with my stories and told me their own. I especially think of the online Facebook magazine readers on *Hold My Hand*. Real, raw, and rare... the courage you gave, shared, and received. This one is for you.

# INTRODUCTION

ALL OF US are storytellers and writers. Our stories show up in day-to-day living, from thinking to doing, and even in imagining and creating. We tell ourselves what we believe, hope, and long to hear. We rehearse themes in our lives... themes like love, forgiveness, hope, and going forward.

No story is complete without you, the writer. *The Stories We Write* is about you. You will find yourself somewhere in this book; perhaps in many places. These writings are a collection of stories I shared while I wrote for online magazines like *Hold My Hand*, *Women as Visionaries With Lore Raymond,* and various other places.

I have arranged this book by themes... twelve of them. Each theme resonates with a description by picture or quote with a collection of stories about that theme. As you read, consider the theme and gather one point from it and carry it in your heart and mind. The morning is often a great starting point to find encouragement and the close of the day lets you continue to "write" in your heart and mind... your own new and powerful stories.

The cover is from my photography of special places where I lived my story, but the messages I've written inside are for the recognition that you have a story, too. It's of a beautiful, God-given life, only you can tell. This book is to be read with hope and inspiration. We all continually learn and grow, and all our stories are in process. Be kind to your story. It's what you give to the world.

~ Summer 2015

# TABLE OF CONTENTS

# THEME I

*Love is worth everything you have, everything it took,
and everything you found.*

~ Carolyn Flinn McCool

**THERE IS LOVE**

THERE MUST BE nothing that keeps you back from telling someone you care. If it's not in your personality, change. Make it important because it is important. Your love has the power to change outcomes. People grow from love. People find hope from love. People get up after being down from love. People find purpose with love. Why would anyone not want to use that power for another's good and their own joy?

### *Love others for the joy and goodness of love.*

Love them just because they are who they are.

Love them for being in your life.

Love them for all they add to your existence.

Love them for what you learn from them.

Love them for the kindness they bring to you.

Love them when the day is going well.

Love them through the challenges and not so well moments.

Love them and let them know it.

### *Tell them. Show them. Display your affections. Write your thanks.*

In our society, I often read things that tell people, with poor self-worth, to love themselves, and then they will feel good about who they are. While I do believe we should learn to deeply love ourselves, and that love works in our hearts to shift us to a new level of acceptance, I also think there is much more to self-respect and valuing your own life. It is not only what I get for myself that I find my worth, it is in what I offer, without return, even though I believe each of us has worth, period. This is a hard concept, because we associate value with certain things, and I believe it takes years of varied experiences to get an appropriate perspective on love and value.

I see so many descriptions of love, but love is not just a description; it is our daily doing and beliefs, which are good and true, for others and ourselves—some of which may even be a hardship for someone (if you have kids you will get this).

I think the point is that we don't always understand love and it is often because our kind of "love" is conditional. It is something I have admitted to myself over the years: that my love is frequently far too conditional, or dependent on what pleases me. The message for me is that my heart needs to get familiar with unconditional love.

Unconditional love is a God-thing. Realistically, no one can love unconditionally without the touch of grace. Unconditional doesn't mean we don't have standards or believe that just anything goes. What kind of child would you raise if you just let him/her do whatever was in his/her heart? A confused one, most likely.

It is unconditional love that makes beautiful, long and lasting marks, but then I wonder, *"Does unconditional even need to be a word accompanying love?"* Love is all-inclusive in its own explanation but we often give it other words to describe and measure it, like "true" or "deep." I have learned that anytime I add words or adjectives to describe love, I often shift away from understanding the nature of unconditional love.

*The hunger for love is much more difficult to remove than the hunger for bread.*

~ Mother Teresa (1910 – 1997)
Roman Catholic religious sister and missionary.

# *The Bread of Love*

SOME OF US are very hungry. We don't need another meal; we don't need a refrigerator of groceries or a pantry of cans. We could use something more filling—and that is love. Psychologists have expressed love as one of our most basic needs. Research has even shown that some animal babies can die from rejection and lack of love. We are not all that much different. We might 'die' in a different way. We might know rejection early in life and it causes us to stumble along to gain our bearings, to feel worth something and valuable. It is very hard when love has been skimpy in our childhood.

Psychology studies report that our brains become wired by our loving or unloving connections. Our nervous system is responsive to touch and to emotional contact. We even talk of bonding when we have a new baby, which brings us to a place of deep respect, love, and connecting. Love is essential to our health.

5

We are here. We are the people we are today. We can't undo what we didn't get. We can mourn some of those losses, but we will lose the wonder of life if we continue in our mourning. We can do something now. We can 'feed' love to those in our charge, to those around us, and to those who are hungry in our reach and influence. In feeding, we also are fed.

Home is such a great place to start and sometimes it is one of the most needy places. We take each other for granted and expect too much, too soon, and too long. Parents get exasperated with their children over normal childhood growth and behavior and are harsh and unloving.

Spouses or friends often hold grudges and never move forward with their obstacles, leaving many doubts to each other, whether they are truly loved. Sometimes, people who are most difficult are just hungry. They are crying out to be loved; they have the hunger pains of love.

Remember to feed your children well but remember they need nourishment beyond bread. The people closest to you in life may have enjoyed a good meal but they may still be starving for the food of love. May they not remain unfilled by your hands and heart because you know love.

*I think it is all a matter of love; the more you love a memory the stronger and stronger it becomes.*

~ Vladimir Naboko (1899 – 1977)
Russian-American novelist\

# I Remember You

SOME PEOPLE WE can't let go. We won't and we can't. Let's face it... there are just some very strong connections for us. Some of those connections are with people we presently live with, and some are with those we wish we could share another day. Some of those people are living and some of them have left this world. We want to remember because we have a piece of them... and we do hope that they have a piece of us. We can't understand everything about the life we live, who and why comes into our lives, or even who goes. It is just how life runs; we come to see how life happens.

When we think we cannot grab and hold onto whomever we love in the way that binds us to them, we can always remember. We can remember what we shared: the smiles, the good times, the trying ones, and the connections. Many memories are sweet to us and in remembrances we find we remember again, and often those who were far somehow now seem much closer. Love feeds a memory and starves our pain, if only a little.

# A Worth It All Kind of Life

I AM NOT done yet. I am still here. I don't have a clue what tomorrow will bring. I am planting seeds, every day, of things I wish for life to bring up but I don't know what kind of storms may be forecasted on my dreams, hopes, and every day. I don't know if I will have flooding rain, fair skies or scorching sun. I don't know but I do know, or at least I deeply desire to believe, though I have uttered things under my breath, it is worth it all.

Some of the hurts we face can make us question the thought of 'worth it all.' I think that is just plain real and honest. I surely haven't figured life out, nor do I really want to. I find it is beautifully lived in trust and with the worthy conviction that it is indeed, 'worth it all.'

Think about love and loving. We were made for this. Oh, yes, it is tough on that heart of ours, and our gray-matter brain, but love is deeply engrained in what we need, want, and search to have. It comes at a price. Love always carries a price tag. Nope, it won't be dangling on the person you love, so you know the suggested retail, but love does have a price tag.

In order to experience love's fullness, we enter a rather vulnerable zone. What exactly, then does vulnerable mean? It means to live with the possibility of being wounded, to be open or exposed for who and what you are. Doesn't sound very comfortable to me, does it to you?

I was vulnerable to cliffs, cacti, and rocks yesterday as I climbed up a steep and unforgiving mountain. It was over the cliff for me, with very little mistakes possible to be made, as I stepped up that beautiful walk. Why would I do that? I would because it is worth it!

Being vulnerable to the mountain stretched and tested me. I saw that I could push through my fears and overcome them and then, relish in my success and joys. Love is much like this.

It does seem there are cliffs and narrow passes on the way, but love will work in your soul. It would be more painful to shrivel up and not go than to carry on and love, but, yes, there are risks when you go out and are vulnerable. If I were to have fallen, it might have been a great injury or death for me.

Love is like that, too, or at least it feels like that when it has offered you a fall. Vulnerability in love, like the risk of climbing a mountain, offers you the potential for both hurt and joy. If you find hurt, you can think it must not be worth it, but consider the possibility you would be wrong. If you find joy, nothing will seem to matter but the effort you gave to love. The world spins on love, never mind gravity and all the science terms. Love takes place in some shape and form at every point in your life on a daily basis; it needs to be there. Don't let one person, one event, one sorrow, one misfortune, one strong emotion or thought, make you choose against love because of a possible risk in loving.

The path may be rocky and steep, or sometimes easy; sometimes the offering of ourselves discourages us, but it is worth being vulnerable, and being known... to ultimately enjoy the power and purpose of love.

## *It's Always Mine*

I DON'T THINK you have lived until you have had a broken heart. I don't think you understand some things until you have been faced with the piercing stab of what you feel when it happens. I don't think you can even love anyone, aright, unless you have had a broken heart. It's not that you don't love or can't love, but there is a place where brokenness takes you... a place where, if you can release and let go, you will learn to fly.

I continue to learn that what and whom I let go actually remains forever mine. Oh, I may not have them in the way I want to, because I have ceased to tamper with what might happen in their journey—and my own. I am learning the art of release. I am aging, and that alone asks me to release some things. I am a parent of grown children and their growth has asked me to release... which began the day I knew I was pregnant.

See, we don't own anyone. We don't own our spouses, friends, children, or anyone we have in our lives. They are free and we must let them be free, to come to us and to love us. Sometimes we have to suffer a broken heart to practice releasing. We are then free to love others for what is, not what we want it to be. There is freedom in release and it changes the way your heart responds; the next time you have an experience you think will break it, that very experience may heal it.

## *Made For This*

I LOVE TALKING with my children; we have funny talks and serious talks, and everything in between. This is one common theme I repeat in my words to them... *Honor God,*

*Love Your Life, Do Well To Others, Life Is Humbling and Short*. As growing adults, I even recently told them this, again.

Today is your best day; believe it! Don't think you have to wait until tomorrow to find it. I know, I get down, too. I have days, well, now, more like moments, when those feelings wash over with a whisper, and I think, *"It's not so great, is it?"* or *"It's not worth it."* I have learned that those thoughts deserve an answer. Ignoring them seems to let them speak their own blasting message, while speaking to them allows me to unwrap and inquire of them.

To love is worth being here. To be loved is worth being here, too. Diminishing your wants is one way to have less with which you are disappointed, but we all have natural human wants. Love is woven in the fiber of our wants and desires.

Honestly, I believe this is a secret to living: simply and easily love life and others just for themselves. Appreciation comes so easy with this line of thinking. I experience this myself as well. For it is true, letting go is a part of all our living and loving. I know this is often hard, but it is also helpful to invest in what you have and what matters. May that be how you find your day, every day, or may you course correct when you have gotten off path. Invest in what matters and trust how life comes to you.

# *Never Blind*

THE GREAT QUOTE, "Love is not blind, it sees more, not less. But because it sees more, it is willing to see less (anon)," presents an interesting view of how we envision others. When we care about another, we will find far 'less' to be irritated by and we will wish them well. We will do all we can to secure the 'well' for them. We are happy for them, not striving to be against them. We understand the holes that might trip us up within a relationship, and we strive to not fall in them. When we cannot wish another well, it is fairly obvious the relationship is heading in another direction.

Speaking heart to heart, not head to head, in matters, is how relational conflicts are mended. They may not solve everything, as situations are difficult, but they address the need of the soul. Just reflect on every conflict you have or have had with someone. If you have met at the heart, you will have understanding and hope. When we speak from our minds to another, the seeds of compassion are often hidden, even if they are there. Only when we can say, "I will listen to what your heart says before I will tell you something," can there be union in conversation.

Heller Keller was blind but absolutely **saw** more than many with eyes. Her writings **inspire** me; one who can see. Enjoy speaking heart to heart and expand what you will see when you present yourself to love!

# *Because I Love You*

THE INTERESTS OF children must be high. They are worth it, though raising children is not as easy as the notion of it is. "You suffer so they won't have to," I say... and have learned. When they are small, you walk slower because their steps are shorter. You adjust your sleep and actions because they ask that of you. You can't do for others and hurry all the time — children teach us that. When they are growing, at times you are inconvenienced in your steps to help them, when you take them places or let them do things that might even be difficult for you. When my son asked me if I loved him, after he had done something that didn't please me, I could only reply, "I may not like what you have done, but there will never be a day when I don't love you."

*"To be wronged is nothing, unless you continue to remember it."*

~ (Kong Qiu) Confucius (551-479 BC)
Chinese teacher, editor, politician, and philosopher

# NOTES

# THEME II

*Forgive. Don't hold yourself hostage to regrets. Notice
what is precious and
good in your life.*
~ Carolyn Flinn McCool

## THROUGH FORGIVENESS

# *I Forgive You*

THERE ARE EVER so many takes on forgiveness and each of us have a particular view we hold. Some of us are generous forgivers, others can be careful forgivers, and some are downright stingy with their forgiveness! Can that be possible? Is that the true nature and extent of forgiveness?

I have been on both sides of the forgiveness experience and each side is a call to growth and love. Our mental wellness is deeply wrapped into forgiveness; sometimes I don't think we see it as such. Harboring ill will for others or even ourselves is defeating, tearing away at our souls and bodies, over time.

One way to be more forgiving is to be less demanding of others, less expecting of them, and less offended by them. When we are 'less' in these areas, conflict is often reduced both in others and us.

Also, as we get older, we begin to see people and life in a different light. We often realize life is not as simple, or as complicated, as we previously created it and understand other people do not always think or do as we do.

Every day is a day that can be opulent in forgiveness, which becomes a richly healing ointment. The holidays are often a reminder to us of our grudges or our graces. They bring up our love or our irritations for those near or around us. Tell someone this season that you forgive him or her. Tell yourself that, too, while you are in the giving spirit. What a gift that would be to give or receive!

## *They Don't Know*

IS THE QUESTION then, "WHAT IS forgiveness for?" I have heard people say they would just never be able to forgive so-and-so, following a discomforting or hurtful experience. It's true some things can happen and you can feel like that, but what does the angst and anger do for you... really? With this frame of mind, you are wounded greatly and will keep putting the spear to your side, to only wound yourself again.

In all my years of life, and they are many, I haven't seen anyone who really got ahead by holding another person hostage to unforgiveness—even those who had a claim and right to do so. There was no movement toward peace, joy, and purpose, that is. You can live yet be a walking dead to the pulse of the world person, and we both know you were made for more than that.

When we can't forgive... it signals work needs to be done in our heart, so we can learn life's lessons; I find these lessons show up to shape us up. Oftentimes, the reality is that someone who can't forgive is actually suffering. Did you ever think of that? We can't know everything that goes on in someone's heart but so many times, they hurt deeply with the kind of hurt that won't go away until they make peace through forgiveness—or we make peace—if we are the one hurting.

The best revenge is to live your life well. It is human to want to be liked and respected. It is human to want the truth to be known about you but that is really not your business, if it does not happen on your terms. I believe you must do what needs to be done to secure your reputation but you must always remember your reputation is more than what others see. It is what you truly are.

*Revenge is a confession of pain.*

~ Latin proverb

# *I Release You*

I will believe the best of you.

I am not angry.

I am not bitter.

I will not hate.

I do not seek revenge, in action or thought.

I let go of what holds me down.

I am free.

Love makes me free.

Forgiveness makes the path smoother.

Kindness gives me peace.

Hope gives you and me a tomorrow.

# *Forgive Me*

SOMETIMES, FORGIVENESS AND the 'process of it' doesn't go so well. Not everyone receives your heart, nor do you quickly receive someone else's. Sometimes, I have learned, I have hurt others and it was hard for them to forgive me. I have learned I can't minimize the wound, especially when it is not my own.

What another carries and perceives is where their work is and I must respect that. There are times an offense can majorly wound others, through both omission and commission. Time cannot be under-played in these instances; in order for the process of connecting and forgiveness to return hearts to a better state. I have learned that forgiveness can be as hard or as easy as we make it, but there are times that real wounds take real work—over an extended period of time.

# *That Offends Me*

OFFENSE IS EVERYWHERE in life. You probably won't go a day with hearing it, seeing it or being involved in it. Sometimes it is given on purpose and at others it is truly unwarranted. You can tell a lot about yourself by how much offense you hold or let go. I enjoy sitting at the feet of the aged, who have learned how to let offense go, and live. It is often youth who struggles with offense and does not recognize the gift it can be.

Offense comes to tell you, you are focusing on the wrong things or people. It comes to say, "You would do well to proceed in a state of humility!" It also asks you if you will chart your own path instead of allowing offense to make you trip all over someone else's. Get smart; live smart.

Offense is like stoplights on the road. They are there to have you pause before you move forward. When you experience offense in your life, you don't barrel through, just as you wouldn't barrel through a stoplight. You see what is before you... you stop... and then you gather your thoughts and feelings before you proceed.

## *When Someone Withholds Forgiveness*

THERE ARE TIMES we wish we could take back what we had done or what we had said. I dislike reading some of the posters I see, and strong stances people take with words and actions of what others do to them. Okay, I so get it, but tell me, would you be the first one to raise your hand and say you had never once said something wrong or did something ill to another person?

If you respond with a "Yes," I am worried for you! You must not be human. Humans have great capabilities and powers for good, but they also can hurt one another... and hurt they do. I talk to a lot of people. I would venture to say this is more the norm for people. I don't know what it is, perhaps I have a sign on my head that reads, "Talk to me, I am safe and

I will listen," but I have strangers tell me their deepest sorrows.

I once took a walk in my neighborhood and saw a lady walking a few streets down from me. I did not know her; she did not know me. She was having a bad season in her life and for some reason I said a few words of greeting and she joined me in the direction I was walking. Now, I often walk for an hour or more, so we were together for a while.

Very quickly the conversation turned to her family heartbreak and struggle. I listened and then I gave her some perspective I had which I thought was helpful. She was so happy to rehearse her pain with a stranger.

I do think many people enjoy unknown company to relay their concerns. I have many strangers who tell me things I don't believe they even tell their nearest and dearest friend. Sometimes it just takes some outside person, who doesn't know you, and you won't see again, to whom you can tell your most heart pressing emotions.

Most of the people I talk to have struggles with others or something they have done in their past, which still filter into their today. One can say they have forgotten the past; a divorce or poor action they once took, but their child, who must now live with daddy or mommy, sometimes has struggles with the two-house arrangement.

Does the person you just blasted or bullied among their peers live with fractured thoughts about themselves? Hurts don't stop when you leave them behind. That is just honest and real, though we must declare they officially do not reign over us.

We often do this through the use of forgiveness. Forgiveness is simple, yet hard. Simple, because it can happen almost with a snap of the fingers for one person to be there; hard because sometimes one or both people are not there, making it appear it will not happen any time soon. Since I talk with so many people about this type of pain, I want you to know this about forgiveness: there is a need for it and a need to give it (this is for me, too). The following is a letter to someone in a forgiving—or the need for forgiveness—struggle:

"I want you to understand that every one of us has failed someone. We have even failed ourselves. It is often only a matter of degree. It hurts and some of us are far more sensitive, causing it to hurt even more. What has often comforted me in my deepest grief is to understand life is full of difficulties and complexities, even when your heart is good and you mean well. Sometimes, though, our own heart is not good and it is angry. Hurt, lots of it, comes from this type of heart.

The person you hurt has hurt others, though they may be short sighted about it. They need a bridge of forgiveness, and one day will need it, with someone they are currently denying, which just may be you.

Sometimes an offense does dissolve a friendship or relationship, and that becomes our reality. We must let things fall as they will, but with the best heart we can give or leave things... to prevent more problems, or agree to just go on. Life is not for torturing you with guilt; I most assuredly believe that is wrong thinking. Heaven knows, we can feel guilt for years over something we have done, where we have tried to make amends, but someone chose to hold out on us, or we chose to torture ourselves. I can understand this, but holding a grudge against yourself or another really gets you—or them— nowhere.

After you make an honest confession and asked the person what you can do to mend the relationship, leave and rest from it, with a measure of grace applied or asked. I know... this is the hard part. We love to punish mistakes and others may love it, too. We really do... as if punishing makes things better. We often regret our actions and they can't be taken back, but they can be worked through over time. You will grow and so will others.

It may hurt... probably will, but remember things happen in other hearts over time. We don't always know how someone is progressing with forgiveness, even ourselves.

People who choose to be hard and unbending to others have their own issues and work to go through. That is their life lesson, even if they were wronged and they are "innocent.," they are responsible for their response.

You can only be responsible for your own actions and words. You will not do it perfectly (the process of forgiving) and neither will others, but if we have a kind eye toward life and others, we will learn in the moment and seek to be better and do better in the future. That is so much what life is about and asks of us. Again, would anyone who is perfect and flawless in this process, please stand up?

There... we all need work, continual work, on the words and actions we take that bring harm to others and to ourselves.

Everyone travels this road, and the one who has been there and knows the pain hurt causes, will be even more watchful to not hurt anyone again. Everyone needs to walk across the bridge of forgiveness, if not today, then someday. Those who can't forgive will continue to be tested—to forgive or engage in conflict—and those who do will teach others how to do it.

The person you hurt needs time and space, after you have offered peace and an apology. Don't assume another's thoughts... just keep having an open heart. Broken relationships will always be some of the bitterest pains in our lives; they test all of us, deeply. Trust that you remain faithful to mending what you can, and also trust that over time healing will happen in quiet places.

## *I Approved This Message*

WE HEAR THE words 'let go' so often we then begin to wonder, "How?" I love picture illustrations; one I often use is the letter and a mailbox. Did you ever drop a letter in a mailbox? It's pretty hard to get it back, isn't it?

There are times I have thought, *What if I really wanted a letter back that I mailed, as in, if I changed my mind about one I sent?* Well... I am not getting it back. I guess I could go to the post office and plead but that probably won't help; it has been sent. Now we can retrieve an email sent, but a letter is a better illustration here.

I think the thought of 'letting go' is a lot like this... you send something away. We all have the need to... send things away. Sometimes it is an attitude that harms us, a person that is not out for our good and best interests, or a habit that is really brings us down to the point we actually hold ourselves hostage. We all know things often take more than will power but our will is always a part of our choices. Then if we go about our life and remember that once we chose to let go, we 'sent something away' and it is no longer with us. That thought, or action or thinking, helped me begin again as I made a pact of peace with myself.

This process applies to our mistakes, our sins, and our failures. I know sometimes we have belief systems at play that hinder this. For some, it is how they view or have been taught about God. I say this delicately, as I know each of us has personal convictions... be gracious and think outside the box. I once was very severe in my thoughts and actions    until I realized that I might have understood a principle in a harsher light than it was ever meant. I have come to believe that the punishment we put upon ourselves so often comes from our own wrong 'thought systems.' That belief... well, it took me awhile to get there, so please be gentle with the process of your life as you grow and go. There is more grace in this place than you can imagine. Grace to let go... and live!

# *Grace For New Places*

I smiled at the lady who sat across from me at the airport terminal. I then asked her how she was doing and where she was going. "San Diego," she said, and I replied that I was headed to Sacramento. We both had about an hour before departure, and I told her why I was going and she with me her reasons for travel.

This woman, in her 70s, began to tell me a most wonderful story. Even today, I could almost cry, as I was deeply touched when she told it. "I am going to see my sisters," she said. "I was given up for adoption and just found my birth mother and I have three other sisters," she happily remarked. "We took a cruise last year and now we are getting together for vacation," she continued.

"Wow!" I said with wide eyes. "That must be awesome, but isn't is hard that it was so long, and didn't you wish you had them sooner?"

"No, I am so happy to have found my birth mother, even now, and I understand her story. She was in crisis and I was given to a great family. I have had a good life. I have no bitterness and I am going forward with happiness," she said.

I sat there, with my mouth opened, but it was only internally open... she couldn't see my thoughts. I kept

27

thinking, *Could I be so kind and forgiving? Would I be bitter or happy?* She then told me the kindest and most endearing thing—and then I was deeply affected and I am crying now as I write to share with you.

"When my mom and I were on the cruise, she brought me gifts for all the special times like birthdays and holidays when she could not give them to me, but she had purchased and saved them over time, and showered me with her love when them to me on the cruise."

I was undone. I saw forgiveness; I saw hope, and I felt it all. She proceeded to tell me how grateful she was and how much fun it was to have sisters, and how it had brought her so much life, today. She was not bitter... she was accepting; and she was forgiving as she started a new life. She chose the better way; she was my lesson and thanks.

# NOTES

Carolyn Flinn McCool

# THEME III

*I hate to complain.*
*No one is without difficulties, whether in high or low life,*
*and every person knows best where their own shoe*
*pinches.*

~ Abigail Adams (1744-1818)
the wife of John Adams and the mother of John Quincy Adams

## THE STRUGGLE IS FOR SOMETHING

# *The Comfort of Life*

EVERYONE IS SUBJECT to the rain of life. We all get wet when it rains. We all have irritations. We all have things that chaff and rub us. This is real life.

What I might find easy to deal with, you might find difficult, and vice versa. There are individuals who deeply love someone whom another person would find unable to bear. Then there are others who truly are not highly offensive, yet someone finds their slight differences extreme. Life... it is easy to feel rubbed the wrong way by it, by other people, and by our own person.

It you wear shoes that are too tight, what do you do? Do you keep walking in them? Some do. Some go and get another pair, either by changing into other shoes they have or purchasing a pair. I did this recently. I am on my feet a lot and my feet did not like my shoes. I changed and bliss arrived. My feet are happy again!

If you know an area in your life that brings you to irritation, prepare and work around it. If you miss sleep and know you will be irritated—why keep missing sleep? If you know that criticism is hard for you, why hide and run from it or feel it is your fault. Instead, watch for things and events that trigger your feelings. Psychology identifies triggers with the senses... smell, sight, etc.

When you learn what triggers or 'pinches' you in life, you have embarked on understanding and the ability to change. This is where you can talk with others about irritations and especially with yourself. When you know something now, you will do better later. The comfort of life is found in working with our irritations and doing what we can with them. Sometimes there will be nothing we can do. Other times, we will come to see our irritations are the gifts and impulses that tell us to try again or do something different.

# *Relax*

WHO WOULD YOU be if you could relax? If you could trust the day and the process, what would you look like? Last week I rode in the desert with friends. We were far from civilization on the ride but as we got closer to the barn the horse I was riding sensed something. I could feel it, first in his body's tension. Then I saw the multi-colored bicycle riders.

My friend's horse, which I was riding, doesn't see multi-colored suited people very often, so she asked us to proceed carefully. I was comforting my horse and being watchful as we went down the hill. As we came upon the cyclers, things proceeded calmly and we asked them to talk to us to calm the horses, since they weren't use to such strange sights. Then they left. Little did I know we would meet them again shortly thereafter. As we neared home, my horse gave off that tense feeling again and all of the sudden halted abruptly. Sure enough, the cyclers were there and startled the horse I was riding. We proceeded slowly again—and peace and calm returned.

How similar, I thought, is life like this for us. We approach something with fear and worry—and sometimes we freeze at it. Frequently, it is really nothing, or minor at worst, and we would have done far better to relax. As a mother I get this. I know my instinct was good when things concerned my kids, but sometimes I could take the tense trail and progressively get tight in the neck and shoulders. I keep learning to trust the process of life more and my reward is to experience relaxation from life. I so love this quote by Martha Beck, "Every obstacle is just an invitation to relax." I think I get it... now.

## *Working For You*

SO MANY TIMES we grieve and think there is no ultimate purpose in our grief. We are so sure we are undone or cast aside to a life we wouldn't want to live. Inch by inch we move forward and the days pass, and sometimes, just barely.

We learn. We learn that maybe some of the hard things that happened to us happened 'for' us as they were happening in us. We see that strength grew out of weakness, faith came up out of fear, and gain realized from losses. We don't know how. We don't know when, but things did come to us. It's not always that life is bad around us; it's more often that we don't see the good near us. Keep looking. Keep going.

## *It's Not Only What Happens To You*

IT IS NOT your obstacles that alone will define you. We are not only what happens to us. The same sun on your shoulders may tan you, but burn me if I do not take care with its power. The power of an obstacle is often in the palms of your hands and the impression you write on your heart.

We each can decide how we will let the things in life touch us and make us feel. This is no place for the weak or the timid. It takes strength to stand up to the challenges on the journey. We are then asked to show up and make something beautiful out of the gracious resources we were given.

## *Don't Cheat*

PLEASE, DON'T CHEAT yourself out of the struggle. The butterfly would not have been able to flap its wings without the struggle and we would not have seen its beauty. Oh, you, your beauty comes out from the struggle. Take a look! Have your noticed it? You are wiser today, aren't you? You are stronger today, aren't you? You are more daring and less afraid today, aren't you? You believe more and doubt less, today, don't you?

Why do you think we love seeing someone meet and defeat an obstacle and rise up in competition? I believe it is because we are made for the challenge. We were made to conquer. We get things we could have no other way. Ease will not give you a strong and resourceful life. It will not get you a loving life.

You will hardly know who you are if you live in constant ease. It is the fire that draws out the impurity and the false, in order to make you strong and pure. Don't cheat yourself out of the struggle. Growing is a gift of life.

# *No Hands*

WHEN I WAS younger I use to love to ride my bike with no hands! I could do it and I thought that was so cool. I have tried recently but I am no longer steady and it doesn't come as easily as it once did. Today I handed someone some papers I needed to be taken from me, and nothing happened.

Time went on, though it was probably only a few seconds. The thought flashed through my mind, *Mister, you could help me out if you would just hold the papers I gave you.* He just seemed disinterested to take them. Then I looked down and noticed he had no hand, or very little of one. I was immediately humbled and recognized I felt more tenderness for him. I also realized I had just asked someone to do something they could not do. I think he was hoping I would lay the papers before him, not hand them to him, as the papers hovered just above the table.

As I departed, I thought, *sometimes we give things to people and they don't give back, not because they don't want to, but they can't or they are unable or uncertain.*

It's like a wife, expecting her husband to know how she feels about things he doesn't get, or a child to understand some of their responsibilities before they are mature enough to do so, or when we expect a certain response from someone and they don't give it.

There are just times others do not have an ugly heart or perhaps they do want to be responsive, but can't or have some difficulty that diminishes their capacity to connect and understand. I don't know why it hit me this way but it probably did because I was wondering what was wrong with this person holding out on taking something from me... when there was nothing wrong with him in the courtesy standpoint; it was that he couldn't physically make the exchange.

Remember those who you love and are connected to you, and when things don't seem to go well, sometimes, others are really trying.

I know of men who feel they can't please a woman, yet they are trying. I know of kids who feel the same about their parents. Don't let someone leave your presence thinking you will not be pleased with them; try to understand the heart, if you don't the hand. That was my lesson today. I am learning.

# NOTES

Carolyn Flinn McCool

_____

_____

_____

_____

_____

_____

_____

_____

_____

_____

_____

_____

_____

# THEME IV

*Traveling with gratitude;*
*find it everywhere.*

~ Carolyn Flinn McCool

# I SAY THANK YOU

## Have You Noticed?

HAVE YOU EVER just taken the time to notice small things? I was at the beach this week and watched a small boat come in from the ocean; the water trickled from its bow down to the sand. Kids were building sand castles and boogie boarding. Have you ever watched a wave form? I watched it gather, then spiral, and spill. It was an amazing display of order and power.

I met a lady who was looking for rocks that were smooth and worn from the rough waves, and I helped her collect them. I even found the coolest pinwheel rainbow seashell.

I was in the mountains not long ago. I watched the clouds move. I watched them go. Coming down the mountain pass, I watched snow fall on it. I watched for all the different flowers as I hiked the mountain trail. I watched for bears, too; Mom always wants me to watch for bears.

Mostly, I watched for love this week, to give and receive. I saw it in the help people gave me and embraced my thoughts, *there's so much love to see in noticing the small things!*

## Some Good Stains

THERE ARE THINGS that happen to us, which can leave a stain on our soul or heart, just like a stain can be left on our clothes. It may merely be a mark that we see and later recall the precious time spent with someone, or it could be a harsh reminder of something gone very wrong.

Time, however, often relieves these stains... as we decide to endure or to keep. How thankful I am for time! It reminded me this week that I owe it so much. I have 'stains' on my bureau dresser that remind me of joy. My twin son chewed on the drawer one day and the teeth marks are still very noticeable... from that once very small mouth. I haven't fixed it. I don't want to fix it. I want the 'stain.'

I am also learning how to live with other stains in my life; things I once felt had to be fixed. Sometimes our stains are there for the remembering... that we have gotten through things, that we have learned a great truth, or even celebrated a moment. Thank you, life, for teaching me that 'as is' is valuable, too.

## *Go And Live In Gratitude*

WORRYING MAKES YOU ineffective, even if you think you are using effective methods of doing something. Oh, you may get things done, but you will more than likely not enjoy the process. If you are having a holiday celebration and your heart is overly full of care, will you actually enjoy your guests? Will you complain and be crabby for what you have to do?

When I was first married, my maid-of-honor shared this with me when I visited her in Houston, Texas, on a trip across the country to get to my new home. After dinner there were lots of dishes, as she was quite a good cook and used many dishes. I offered to help, but she said, "I am leaving them. I want to enjoy and savor your company. Then, when I do them, I will think of the good time we had." That thought has remained in my mind each time I have entertained—and there has been lots of entertaining over the years.

Now, sometimes people pitched in and helped, and there were times, I said, "Sit down, and I am sitting with you. My dishes are not as important as you." I have never regretted that choice and point of view. There are times I have done dishes for a good stretch of time, but it has been with a grateful heart that I had friends and family—and I had the health and strength to do those dishes. Some may say that is inefficient, but when it comes to loving, some rules or methods just don't apply.

Many times, after we have shared special moments with others, we say goodbye to them. In fact, we often have many events in our lives when we say goodbye to people we have spent time with or who are leaving us. Goodbyes are not easy, but they are significant moments in the way we leave others. I remember when I would travel to see my family, who lived across the country, for the holidays. It was such a time of anticipation, even weeks before the event. I can recall some of those flights 'home' and greetings at the airport or even at their front door.

Oh, those were sweet and honest moments. I remember crying many times upon departing their presence, and so did they. As I would leave and wipe my tears, I would board a plane or drive off in a car and then cry some more, even if not outwardly. Sometimes I would pass by strangers and think, *No one knows my heart but me*. One thing I know I treasure in the going, even in the tears, is to go in gratitude. If you have to go… I say, "Go in gratitude."

*Go in a spirit of togetherness and deep affection.*

*Go walking hand-in-hand with love.*

*Go to your work with the remembrance of the love you have and the love you made. as they lived across the country.*

*Go with kindness for what you experienced and the high notes that keep playing in your heart and mind.*

*Go with your memories to savor long after the day is done or the person is no longer with you.*

Going in gratitude will keep you grateful, as you remember. It will curb your sorrows to reflect and remind you, how much you have experienced. So, go in gratitude; you have been so very blessed and have so much to be thankful for.

## Glitter The World

IMAGINE IF EVERYTHING you were to touch turned golden. You know, King Midas, of Greek literature fame, had that touch. Well, today, someone else has that touch. A man sat down not far from me and I noticed, his wife, date or girlfriend, sat down close to him. Well, it was very close and they began kissing in that near space, not just a little but a lot. Ok, so I noticed! They also had a child with them who looked like she was coloring.

A little time passed and the next time I saw the man, he had glitter above his lips. Wow! Could you imagine what life would be like if every positive, loving, and fun act you did, spread glitter on you and others? It would seriously put you and others on notice that something wonderful had come your way or was shared. I wondered... *How glittered up would I be? How glittered up would you be? How glittered up would our closest ones be? Would it be enough for the world to notice?* So, I am going out to glitter the world. I hope you will join me.

## *Five Myths of Thankfulness*

IF YOU FEED a lie, it will grow; both fact and truth. I constantly ask myself, "When it comes to difficult or conflicting matters, do you have the facts straight and are you seeing things as they are?" This thought brings me to see parts, big and small, and to look more lovingly and factually at a situation.

You know, too much emotion can steer facts and solutions into the ditch. Here are five myths I believe we can hold about thanksgiving... I have held every one of them, at some time:

1. You can't be thankful unless things are going well. This is lie number one, to me. We often plan for a smooth life and then, things don't turn out like we had planned. I am still learning that sometimes, this is the way to an even better path. The truth is, it still is upsetting to have dreams dashed and plans crashed but it is absolutely not true that things must be going well to be thankful.

**Did you look at your hands and see the work they have done for you or count the fingers on your grandchild's hand? Well, see, there are things for which you can be thankful and plenty of them.**

2. You need to have things to be thankful... things such as people, possessions, or position. Wrong again. Granted, things do enhance your thankfulness. I don't know anyone who would not like a raise or find a favorite gift under the tree this year but those 'things' won't keep you thankful. They don't have the power to keep us satisfied. People, even loved ones, disappoint us—just as we disappoint them. Possessions break, wear out or get stolen. Position changes. Someone is on top... and in time they are no longer even anywhere on the ladder. Life is humbling, but there are reasons to be thankful beyond things or positions.

3. You must be secure and certain in your finances and health. That's nice and I would think an important goal to work for, but it's never a guarantee. You can do right and well in life, yet still find yourself out and down. I have learned thankfulness is as much a present appreciation as a continued desire for goodness in your life.

**Health is wealth, as they say, but it is to appreciate what you have now that ranks high. I know all too well about thinking I didn't have things in the past... when I really had more than I believed I did at that present time.**

4. You will only be thankful if your dreams come true. I believe in dreams and I believe they are vitally important because they are so you, so who you are. I just believe that we define dreams in certain ways... and sometimes we can be living a dream but defining it wrong. If I think thankfulness is everything going well but the baby is sick, I am tired, and my husband didn't get the promotion he had his dream set on, then I will struggle to be thankful.

**What if I looked at the gift of the child we have together or the possibility that the missed promotion was just a stepping-stone to another path? Might I be filled with hope and thanks that I was directed in that way?**

5. You must be loved and well liked. On the surface, that looks like you can't possibly argue with that one, but let's take it one step further... Thanksgiving is generally an inside job with gratitude contributed from surprising sources.

Whenever I feel thankfulness is exclusively outside me, I know I am in trouble. I can't navigate or control my response then. However, whenever I believe love is mine... I have been given it, I am it, and acceptance begins with me, I find it easy to be thankful. I am not searching as a gold miner did in the 1850s in California.

**I believe life's best gifts are near me and they are already in my possession, in some shape and form, and gratefulness is a gift, visible or yet unseen, but nearby.**

# *Glorious Day*

I KNOW THE calendar says it will be another year in about 24 hours but the truth is... it is just another glorious day dawning. I don't like to say this was a good year and this was a bad year. Why? Those years are all a part of my life and have shaped me. Do I remember certain things more fondly in some or one of them? Sure, I do.

I can also say my most tragic and difficult years are gifts to me. They taught me how to recover and live. They were as necessary as the 'good' ones. I really do not believe I would love the opportunity for a new day, as I do now, if I had sunshine every day.

Sometimes we look for a year with nothing but easy or 'good' things to happen to us, which just may be our undoing. We have work that needs to be done inside to receive the greater gifts we can enjoy.

My lessons over the years are wrapped up in failing and succeeding; in gaining and losing. Mistakes are such a part of my life and the trying to be so careful not to make them has long passed. I will try. I may fail, but I can receive that because it is not getting there **perfectly** that is so important to me. It is that I attempted—I struggled because I wanted something and I went for it. I tried. I willed. I will not let the world system tell me I only succeed if I accomplished something **it** deems as worthy: make such-and-such amount of money, be with so-and-so, and have this-and-that. I have been many places, with many people, and completed goals... but I can tell you in the last stretch of my life it's not just getting there that has meaning but how I do it, who I lovingly take with me, and why I do what I do!

The calendar date keeps changing, but I am doing the same thing(s) I have learned to do, day after day. That is to present all of me to what I love to do and do it with a full heart. Where it takes me is not always my call. When a farmer plants a crop, do you think he knows the exact bushel amount he will get? Never. Oh, yes, he estimates but so many other factors happen over time, yet, he plants, cares, and goes forward. That is life to me.

There is no magic in a new year that didn't follow yesterday. The magic is in taking care of whatever and whoever is before you. This is what I call magic. Life holds the possibility for mistakes but you still go out and try. You go and live. That is the magic and that is—the opportunity of another glorious day!

## *The Relief*

I DON'T KNOW of any medicine quite like the medicine of thankfulness. It is most unfortunate its effects are often underrated and underreported. No one needs insurance for it, there is no monetary payment, and you don't have to stand in line either to receive it. Gratitude, when coupled with thanks, provides a great amount of healing for you throughout life, if you choose it. Gratitude does not fall down from the stars to change you; it must be invited in and welcomed.

Gratitude begins by just respecting the simple things that are going on in your life or not going on. Can you breathe? Can you feel your heartbeat? Do you see the steps before you? Then it builds, as you begin to list and rehearse what you are thankful for. You can name people, places, projects, and passions that bring you to appreciation. You can even change the way you see the things that will build the level of value in thankfulness.

## *Thank You For Taking Care Of My Heart*

I HAVE TAKEN trips in my life where I need someone's help to watch the animals, check the mail, and do other things I needed while I was away. There is nothing quite like having someone or people in your life who help you do the things you required of you as you enjoy your life. You can count on them to feed the dog or cat you love, to water your grass, check the mail, and most importantly, lock your door! We are better for those who take care of our hearts.

I hope as I write this, you are thinking of those who take care of your heart. I hope, even more, you will be sure they know. I am convinced that someone should know how you feel about that caring. I know when we date or are young we might play a few games and engage in the process of who-likes-who, but don't let that be your standard throughout life. Tell those who take care of your heart you love them.

When I lost my beloved father I will never forget what my sister said to me just after he died. "The world has lost a great man. It is poorer without him," she said. My dad was great to us and he was good to his world. Not everyone loved him like we do and that is fine, but to us he was wonderful.

The reason she had such strong feelings and said what she did was because she lost someone who took care of her heart. He was one less person in the world that would be there for her and us. Love was expressed freely in my family; I heard it in words and saw it in play.

Wear out the words with those you treasure and find new friends and others to whom you can say them. I even say this word to strangers I have had some good interaction with and they beam. Love does not mean only romantic love. I can say, "I love you" because I have a fond caring and respect for you. I know the words are special and should not be thrown around carelessly, but we can love in degrees and ways. It is still love.

Remember those who take care of your heart and tell them! Add to the telling and show them. We love to be remembered. We delight to see, hear, and read love in every form. It does not make you less because you do; it makes you understand its greatness when you respect **love.**

# NOTES

# THEME V

*It's much how I use the eyes that can see,*
*which colors the choices that will be.*

~ Carolyn Flinn McCool

## YOU CHOOSE

# *You Just Know*

SOMETIMES THINGS JUST happen in your life and you know you have changed. You are so rock bottom sure how you see things is drastically different from how you once did-- and you now make different choices. You are standing on the other side of the fence so-to-speak. The old things don't have the same pull anymore. You even find that you can walk away from things or people that once stirred such a reaction in you.

You don't walk away with hate or anger. You walk with an assurance that you have peace and you made a good choice. It's not out of pride but of humility and thanks. It's a gratitude walk of appreciation that you learned something, though it may have cost you dearly, and you have peace as you go forward.

*"Two roads diverged in the woods, and I took the one less traveled by, and that has made all the difference."*

~ Robert Frost (1874 – 1963)
American poet

# *Choose Your Trip*

THERE ARE PLENTY of people who will tell you how to live your life. Someone will make choices for you, if you pass on making them yourself. Sometimes we think we are kind to let other people choose for us, when in reality we are just afraid and insecure. It takes guts and determination to live a life all the way through. It takes courage to live your life by your design... strategically and with pre-determined goals to bring the most of the best of life to yourself and those whom you love.

People who are afraid of making mistakes often let other people decide for them. People who fear another's disapproval often do the same. Until you can change your mind about how you see life and want to see your own life, nothing much will change. Those whose existence is to tell others what to do get in a routine, and become unhappy when others don't want to follow a certain perceived pattern. Breaking poor or old patterns that are not profitable or healthy can be very hard but freeing.

Choose your trip in life... and buy a ticket to the destination you wish to travel. It's far better than letting someone else pick a place for you. Make choices and take steps to get there through hard work and determination. It will be fun and well worth it. It is always worth it to live the life you want to live. Let others live the life they are called to live. It really is a do-it-yourself job... life, that is!

## *Status Update*

I OFTEN CHUCKLE when I read, "What's on your mind?" on the status bar on Facebook. Well... I think about lots of things most of the time. It's difficult to not have thoughts about something. I think that is evidenced by others, as well, and by what is all around us—in the news and our daily dealings.

I know it is no secret that our thinking is important to how we relate to our own life and how we live in this world. We don't live in a vacuum; what we do on the inside, reaches outside of us. Like cause and effect, our lives constantly act as moving forces on others. I once felt helpless to my thoughts, in that I had to live them as they came. I don't believe that at all today. It was not a medicine that gave me that revelation, though I do not despise the help others find in them. It was discipline to think differently. It was just like exercise and getting fit—it involved work and it didn't happen overnight. This definitely doesn't mean I never struggle with my thoughts, either. It does, however, mean I have learned another way to live.

I love the deep association between thinking and feeling. Perhaps you learned this long ago, but a slow learner is still a learner! If I want to **feel** differently, I challenge myself to **think** differently. I can't honestly ask myself to feel what I don't think. I can't tell myself what I should believe in a certain way, if I really believe something else.

This understanding has taught me to respect the difficult places where thought occurs, too. I work to acknowledge the unsettledness of my thinking, listen some, and carry on, waiting for what life will ultimately teach me. The lesson learned is that to ignore or not deal with life, only serves to push peace away. Things will continue to show up later, which boldly ask to be addressed, so why not deal with them now?

# *What Are You Thinking?*

SO, WHAT ARE you thinking? Oh, I don't have to know. There are things that are private and that's great. It's just what you give your energy to, gives life to someone or something. When I complain, it gives life to my complaining. When I walk and talk peace, it gives life to my peace. When I play on my fears, it keeps them alive and I become my fears. When I give life to love, love gives life to me. The great connection of feeling and thinking is so important that I love learning how to live it, write about it, and speak about it, whenever I can. We are headed where we are thinking. So, what are you thinking? Where are you going?

# *Change*

IT TAKES TIME to change; though it is true some things can change in an instant. Sometimes change is happening but we don't immediately see it. Just look at the sandstone or limestone on many mountain cliffs. They are being shaped by the wind and weather through erosion. We often don't actually see the geological changes happening, but in time, we see what has transpired.

This is a good analogy of what often happens with people. We want them to change or we want to see change in our own lives. We feel nothing is happening, but how wrong we are. Underneath and behind what we don't see, or can't see, things are happening. Although change sometimes seems to happen in leaps, it is more frequently accomplished in small, deliberate increments. It's like this when you haven't seen someone for some time, and when you see them again, the first thing you notice is how they have aged. They didn't change overnight, but they definitely changed. On the other side, a child can be sick in bed from a fever or illness, but once it breaks, he/she is up and moving, as in a quick change.

When we fail to bear with others or ourselves, we will miss how they or we might change, and so much of growth is because of change. I think children are an amazing gift for understanding change. We watch them progress from stage to stage. Life is full of change and it's a humbling journey to see a life grow within you and before you.

The wind and the weather take mountains and shape them; they change. They continue to change from erosion and other elements of nature, and people come from around the world to see their beauty in amazement. How much our lives and other's lives are like this as we journey through our changes and they... their own. It can be from birth to death, from crawling to walking, from illness to health or vice versa, from sorrow to joy, and nothing to something.

We know each other through change, and much of the time, through honoring change in others, and ourselves, we discover what has made the other person or our own lives so desirable and beautiful to us.

# *It So Matters*

A FILM PRODUCER said on his deathbed, "Nothing matters. Nothing matters." While I can't be sure about the context of his words, I will leave room for what he might have meant, but I can't let his words go by without comment. If he felt nothing mattered, I would like to have been next to him, holding his hand, and offering him some tender words. So, does nothing matter?

Ridiculous you might say, right? I might have uttered different words like, "Everything matters. Everything matters." One wheel turned moves you further on the road, depending on how quickly or slowly that wheel turns. One kind word, against the harshest and desperate of times, has power that perhaps only the person hearing it knows. One minute can mean catching the train or standing on the platform to wait for the next one. I think of the "starfish experience" and how the tossing back into the water mattered to that one starfish.

Every moment of every day you are doing things that matter. You have choices to make based on who and what you think matters. Your day is arranged based on what matters to you. How you treat the next person is determined by what you think matters. How you will live matters. It all matters. It really does.

# *Watch Your Reaction*

THEY SAY IT takes two to tango. I do and don't believe that... at least in some aspects of life. There are places life will take you where it is not your fault, not your karma, not your own making, and not your doom. Life and the thoughts of reaping and sowing and even karma are general and not specific or exclusive truths in this life.

Now, I also believe nothing comes our way that does not serve us and does something in us for some good and some direction we are asked to travel. I don't like that thought, at times, but I believe in the purposes and designs of life, though I don't even know to what extent or degree. One thing I do know... my reaction matters!

People can rough you up in the battle of words and situations, but what I do, is mine to own, and that is the hard part of life... at least one hard part.

There are people who love to bring others down, verbally, viciously, or in a cold-hearted way, but it is your work to not let them take you there. They may do it subtly or overtly, but you don't need to know why—you only need to know what is in your heart and trust it, and choose the better and the best. We become as guilty as the one who argues or maligns us when we react horribly or unkindly. We really do ourselves no good and it is hardly justifiable to heap evil-back-for-evil or harm-for-harm, but it is done every day in various ways.

Learn this lesson of life... take care of your own heart and listen to it. You will stand **with you** longer than you will stand with anyone else. Walk tall and proud, in a humble way... knowing you chose the honest and best way to walk.

## *Put It In Neutral*

EVERY MINUTE of every day we choose between two emotions: fear and love. We would love to say every action we make comes from love, but we would be dishonest if we said that. We must hope to make many of our choices for love and keep making them... Love—as in kindness, peace, freedom, wisdom, grace, etc.

Fear is the other side of life's coin. Fear sometimes appears easy to flip to or drive toward. This is a good time to 'put it in neutral' when we get in fear's grips and shift gears. I believe it is easy to fear because we do not understand its basic operation. Fear is a thief; it comes to rob you again and again. It surprises you, even when you have good intentions to be ready for it. It is subtle, too, as it plays into relationships and life. It sneaks up on you and says, "I got cha."

Fear comes to you disguised as anger, rejection, doubt, anxiety, unsteadiness, and uncertainty. Fear is not your friend, but sometimes you are wise to sit with it and visit a while.

Someone once did an acrostic on fear and I love this:

**FEAR**
**F--False**
**E--Evidence**
**A--Appearing**
**R--Real**

I know there are some things to fear in life: a hot stove, a poisonous snake, turbulent water if you are near it, and a very difficult and unkind person. You may know other normal and *necessary fears*. This story is not about that. It is about the fears over which we have no control, like: "Will I get cancer? Will my money run out? Will I get through this difficult time? Will my child get a job? Will someone want to marry me?"

So much of what we tell ourselves, when we are in a hard way, is a lie—and we believe it. These false appearing beliefs harm others and us. Fear can paralyze you and cause you to freeze in your tracks—and then do **nothing**— based on false evidence! I want the truth and the truth will not come if I walk with fear—**false evidence appearing real.**

No! I will choose what is true. I have a choice to make every minute between **fear** and **love**. I will choose **love**. I will pray I choose **love** more than **fear**. I know I am human, but I also know I have power. **Love** is where power is—**choose love.**

# *Why I Love The Present*

PLEASE LOVE THE present, dear soul. It is really only what you have. Of course yesterday is yours... all the loves, the joys, the sorrows, the mistakes, and the learning. It could be no less, but today is here to give you more. Don't fear more. More comes to make more of you and your life, not take more out of you.

Today is a gift that will come many times in your life, but one day, it will not show up. Today, the present is where you make your life. Make it a purposeful and happy one, and remember purpose does not merely come for what makes you happy.

Some of your greatest gifts will come to break you, to take from you, and redirect you, so you will find more to live in the present and more to be grateful for. It is how a good life comes. It is how appreciation arises.

Dear Soul,

Today is yours... hands off of yesterday, unless you are thankful for what it has done within you and the lessons that have strengthened you, then it may be looked upon. Don't mourn today. Today wants to show you life! It is time you allowed it to do so!

*We must learn to regard people less in the light of what they do or omit to do, and more in the light of what they suffer.*

~ Dietrich Bonhoeffer (1906 – 1945)
German Lutheran pastor, theologian, anti-Nazi dissident.

# NOTES

# THEME VI

*Growing and thriving are near inseparable;*
*one so often goes with the other.*

~ Carolyn Flinn McCool

## OUR RELATIONSHIPS

## Tell Them

I HOPE YOU never hide your feelings from those you love. People love to be told that you care and they are in your thoughts. One day you may not have another day to tell them.

When I was busy with my kids, there was an older woman who sold honey down the street from me. She had lost her husband and would call and try to connect with me. I did a little for her, but I was mostly lost in my responsibilities.

One day I learned she had died. I felt sad—sad to lose her, and sad that I didn't reach out more. I was too absorbed in what I was doing. It was part of changing the way I saw life... living and doing life. People count on our love and consistent place in their lives. Your love and care is special to someone, just as theirs is to you. Tell them while you have them.

## It Is Not What It Is

ONE DAY AT work I had a customer who wasn't pleased. I had done what I could for him and his family, but he was still not satisfied. He got upset. I told him I would get a manager. The man proceeded to tell my manager why he was upset and we worked something out for him, but not before he got very angry with me and spoke harshly.

My coworker looked on, and after the man and his family were taken care of and out of view, he said to me, 'I feel so sorry for you, the way that man spoke to you." I looked at my coworker and said, "I am good. My heart was able to tolerate that situation because I did the best I could; I am okay. That man will feel different after he cools off." I said a brief prayer and asked God to bless this time and that I would understand the man and not given to anger. I felt compassion for this person who was compelled to lash out at me. About 30 minutes went by and this hand touched mine—it was the man. He took my hand to shake it, and I placed my hand on top of his, as he apologized for his outburst and said he was very stressed and probably was overly sensitive about what happened. I told him, "I forgave you before you even came up to me!"

I saw that man many times after in the course of business, and he was kind to me, as I was to him. It reminds me to go further to understand and to not hold someone, even someone who hurts you, hostage to your own anger. I have not always done this but I am learning.

## *Keeping Ties*

I LOVE ROPES, strings, threads, and dental floss. They all have purposes and uses. They tie things or weave things, together. Symbols often show us things that are together, symbols like a ring or flowers. Ties are good for us, unless they are too tight, such as a businessman's necktie.

Ties can also be difficult for us, but no one can live well without them. To be untied to the good things of connecting relationships is to miss out on what you were made for. Oh, yes, ties grow and stretch you and, sometimes, we want to break them but ties enrich life—others and ours.

Tying your life to others may bring you struggle and challenge, but it will also gain you connection and a future. It will bring you love and smiles and even tears and sorrows... but it will be so worth it in the whole scheme of life.

We must take care of broken things and broken people. We do not know if a similar life place will be our own at some point in time. We must also remember we, too, may have to cross difficult bridges someday. I want to cross those bridges **with** someone. Tying strings and threads, tightly but with space, brings you the opportunity for love and lasting relationships. It is a most beautiful way to live and love life.

## *Bringing Love*

WHEN YOU ARE loved, the one who loves you wants to bring good into your life. It doesn't mean you won't have some challenges when you love or are loved, but when you are loved, your care is vital to the one interested. It's fulfilling and exciting to feel that you are special to someone. Honestly, I don't know one person who doesn't want to be wanted and to be loved—and to be special to someone else.

Parents can be pretty cool at this job. While they are leading and loving, a lot of things happen that often are more clearly understood in the days ahead by the child under their watch today. It's great that parents have foresight, and that is partly because they have lived a while. It's also great that when you love, you want to be good to the one you love. I know… I know, it's not always like the love you imagined, but sometimes the love you share with another far exceeds your wildest imagination.

## *Thinking Of My Best*

YESTERDAY WAS MY dad's birthday, but he is not here to celebrate it. At the time of this writing, it has been five birthdays without the one who is undoubtedly the most influential man in my life. The days, as they unfold, continue to show me what he was teaching me all along. He even showed me how to die. I pray I will use that example when my time comes. We must embrace that love brings precious, and sometimes unusual gifts… doesn't it?

My dad knew how much I loved and was crazy for horses. He often took me to ride at nearby stables where we lived; he rode with me. I have fond memories of riding with my dad who was a good horseman. I think horses were in each of our blood. I remember reading his young brother, Kenneth's, obituary and a brother's words, "He loved cherry pies and wanted to grow up and have a dude ranch." He never grew up, and died very young of brain cancer, but in small ways, dad carried on the love for Kenneth through horses and letting me ride.

One day, it was just my day… Dad let me have my own horse when we were stationed in Colorado. Three years of bliss it was! Colorado Springs celebrates the Pikes Peak or Bust Rodeo. I rode in that rodeo in a drill team called the Austin Bluff Rangers, on a horse he and mom bought for me. I still recall riding my horse down main streets in the parade in downtown Colorado Springs. I was high as a kite on life.

People who love us are good to us. That was how I saw my dad and my mom. They sought to please us and bring in life's delights. It's a beautiful part of life—when someone thinks of your best interests.

## *The Everyday In The Not-So-Ordinary*

TODAY I PICKED up my son from a train station in the rolling hills of New Jersey. The area is serious horse country, with the National Equestrian Center nearby. I was back in the horse country I love. The memories quickened... of dad buying me a horse, when I was a pre-teen, and I was suddenly *home*.

Love is home. But I realize as I write, that many of my joys, as I am sure yours, are from someone loving you. They are from someone doing something for you, for your interest. It might have cost them greatly. It might have been something free, but it was because of love.

Love makes the greatest gift. It creates joy, which gives you what we call a "sky high" feeling, but it can just be the simple thrill of knowing that you are loved. So, I walk in gratitude because it is love that gives us a beautiful life, and it is people who are generous to us, and who often give us a love only found in sacrifice and giving.

It is often just a look or a flash of a memory that reminds us of someone or something we hold dear and the love we have experienced. Who is to say that the every day is not extraordinary?

# *If You Knew*

I WRITE BECAUSE I love to and I write because I want to pass on things I have learned and because I love to encourage and help others. If you knew some skills, today, that would help you have a better life and better tomorrow, would you be glad to know them? Stop reading… if that is not important to you or you know all you need or want to know. But, if you want to learn something, listen and continue along this path.

My cousin, who is a counselor, shared this with me recently and made me realize I will never stop learning: Did you know someone has assigned three stages to marriage? I also think this concept is appropriate for all relationships.

1. **The honeymoon stage**. Here, interest and excitement are high. You are new to the joy of love and marriage, and so is the other party. People are seen through rose-colored glasses and often perceived to do no wrong. Conflict is low and fun is high. A slice of heaven the honeymoon stage can be…

**2. The disillusionment stage.** Here, reality finally comes home; it hits you and your spouse. You see how the toilet paper gets unrolled and how the clothes end up on the floor, or not in the hamper. Here, some of the not so desirable things about us show up. The person we thought we married, is not who we thought they were, and vice versa. It is easy to feel cheated and disillusioned. *This is not what I bargained for*, you think.

3. **The reconciliation stage.** If couples get this far, they can survive and thrive within the marriage. The move through disillusionment can be long or short—it all depends on hearts, habits, and the views held. It also depends on how much grace and forgiveness you will give to someone else. When the reconciliation with what life is and what you wished it to be can be at rest, then real joys can be shared and memories made. It won't mean you quit and lie down, but it will mean you understand and grow through places of discomfort on the way to new comforts and love.

Marriage is a growing investment in yourself and another. It is worth the work it takes to build lives. People often don't like to think relationships are work, but because it is easy to think about your own needs, at the expense of others, it takes effort to focus on another person's needs.

# *Love You More*

MOTHERS OFTEN LOVE, and even live, to be helpful to their adult children. Parenting is not, to me, done for a certain time, after which you are relieved of being a parent. There is probably nothing more rewarding than to help someone or make their life a bit more pleasant, easier or more knowledgeable. We are all busy people with things to do, and sometimes, life seems to scream at us to, "Do!" Even though life is different and my kids are grown, I told my son as he ventured out to life, "I want you to make your way, but as long as I am in your life, I want to do you good, so as you have emotional, physical or material needs, your dad and I will do what we can."

Yesterday while I was with that special young man, waiting to help him with something, I noticed a group of young girls and an older-age woman near me. I learned they were apartment shopping. They were in serious discussion, with smiles and warmth shared between them. I gather that the older woman must have been the mom helping the girls because of the way the conversation was going.

After their decisions were apparently made, the girls and mother parted. As the woman crossed the street, one of the girls shouted out, "Love you." It was just a flash of a second and words flew back. The assumed to me mother responded, "Love you **more**." Wow! That just ticked my heart a few beats higher. **Love you more!**

I love lessons on a crowded New York City street where I am the student. I love when someone reminds or teaches me a gentle and good lesson. Isn't it grand to have people in your life who respond back that they love you more? Isn't it great to tell someone that you love him or her more?

# *I Care*

SOMETIMES WE ONLY get one last time... one last time to speak to someone, to kiss them, to hold their hand, and to be in their presence. We often don't know when that one last time will be.

Take care of your moments. Don't live in an argumentative state with others. Don't keep secrets that wound others. Tell people you love them, need them, and are glad they are there. You may only have one last time, because one day that is what it will be.

# *It's Settled*

THIS IS A long read. Please don't continue unless you want to be challenged in an unconventional way about settling for things in life. The word "settled" goes around a lot these days. "Oh, I won't settle for a relationship like that or a situation like that," I hear. I also hear things like, "She settled for him?"

There are even Facebook posts about deserving to not settle in life. I believe we find more unhappiness in life, with others, and ourselves because we choose not to settle for things we should learn to grow through and be settled in. This is not a popular position often taken today, but I believe it is a truth. This is an observation from an older person, mind you, who has lived a bit, and also from speaking with people, even years older than I am. Why do I feel like this? Four reasons:

1. **We won't take trouble**. We live in a society that won't take anything anymore. Instead, the goal is to find someone to blame, sue, hate, and "dish" on. Since when did the "guaranteed life" ever become the standard of living?

Shall I sue or blame because I got a larger than average nose than someone else? So, if I have a child with a birth defect or disability, is it always someone's fault? If my family was poor while I was growing up and I had to work to go to college, should I hate someone else for that?

The thread of discontent is sewn in thinking you deserve something. People who are close to me know I do not use or like the word, deserve. That, to me, is an arrogant and owning word. Your life is a gift, not a demand or guarantee.

2. **We won't accommodate** others' weaknesses, yet we have our own. I have yet to meet a perfect person, but I have met people who think they are close. You know, the people who try to make you feel small, who remember your mistakes, and who shove others around—but they think that is normal behavior—except when someone else does it to them.

We live too close to ourselves, so we often fail to see our faults or shortcomings. This is why I so believe in marriage and connection. Here is the forum where you will grow! I wrote a letter to a friend, when I was first married, and told her marriage is such exposure.

Little did I know, children are even more exposure. These places are our gifts! In marriage and parenting I got to learn to cooperate, to share space, to love, to forgive, to apologize, and to make peace. Mom had it right, "If you don't get along here, what makes you think you will get along out there!"

I know, family interaction can be rough and those outside — who don't know your faults and foibles may not always be so rough — but family is for a reason, and one reason is to learn to work together and get along. We are better for this growth, though it crosses our wills and is not always an easy way.

3. **We love and ideal.** Oh, I am so guilty of this and I finally can admit it — to myself! We often romance both life and people. People and relationships are not always so pleasant — even those you love and dwell with.

You know, we have to talk about matters to solve them. We have to give up certain things to get others. We have to humble ourselves to admit we were pig-headed and wrong. I wonder — is a pig really pig-headed? I don't know, but I heard that phrase before and I think it means stubborn and unbending.

What's so beautiful about ideals in loving relationships? What will you get for the whole of your life from standing on principle when it is stomping on others or keeping them from you? I am all about preservation of principle and good, but it can be done in a gracious way, when we keep learning and growing in gracious ways. That's part of what our life is for. That's how we can finish well and finish with others.

**4. We think it is all about us.** What we believe about life shows up in how we live. Everyone has a belief system and we each travel with it. One thing I love about life is challenging myself to think differently so I might currently perceive something from a fresh perspective. According to a friend, that's called "Flip the Coin" thinking. Did you ever think how your husband feels after you talked down to him? Wouldn't you be more open to compassion if you did? Did you ever think how your wife feels when she is struggling about something and you want her to stop talking or just fix it? A little compassion might help you hold hands and hearts. Our experience of life is not all about you or me.

It's also not just what you get and how you get it, especially when what you get hurts and harms another along the way. The person who stole the gift cards, which were a gift for my son, from the mail and used them... harmed more than the one for whom the gift cards were intended. The coworker, who took my friend's purse, which luckily was taped on camera, is missing what life is all about. It is not about all you get and thinking you are settling when you don't get the partner, the place, the purpose, and the plan you want. It is very much about taking what you were given and gifting yourself and others... by creating your best self in the place you live. You know, I continue to learn; you can do that anywhere and with anyone.

# NOTES

Carolyn Flinn McCool

# THEME VII

*I will not mourn forever what is gone, though
I will honor what has come and
been taken from me.*

~ Carolyn Flinn McCool

## DISAPPOINTMENT AND LOSS

# *Almost Over You*

"I AM OVER you, if one can ever be over the one they loved and shared their soul and dreams. I am over the anger; loving appreciation for what we shared has replaced it. I am over the 'get even' feeling, caring about your real interests are my only reasons now. I am over waking up like there is weight on my chest and an anvil on my heart that keeps forging pain. I can smile and say, thank you, for all you brought me."

"I am over the bitterness of what might have been and loving what is on the road of gratitude and growth. My thoughts are for you to live a beautiful life in the choices you have made, in the places you will travel, and all the love you will make. I loved. I love. That is the greatest gift of all my sorrows and I am almost over you."

# *We Care*

DAD ALWAYS TOLD me, "It is only the people you love, and want to love, that can hurt you." I know this is not totally true. A stranger can commit a crime against me and hurt me but I think my dad was talking about the hurt in my spirit, from being wounded by those close to me. I think his belief is valid.

I recently spoke with someone about this. Love is not the absence of hurt. I know, in the truest and best sense, love should be gentle and gracious but in the process of it we sputter and stall. I have worked and continue to work along these lines, today, to heal and not wound. We can deeply care for someone and mess up royally trying to remedy a problem or challenge between us. We can say dumb and hurtful things or, sometimes, we can do well and right, and yet get the "bad guy" label—even when our intentions are the purest and best.

Relationships are always tested, and reveal what you really have between each other. Tested, in that you see how much you love and how mature you are. It's easy to say, "I love you," but it is much harder to demonstrate it and keep on doing so. When you are in conflict and the hurt flies, try to step back and look at the other's perspective and not your own. Was an apology given? Have they tried to reach you? They care. Don't assign too high a standard or judgment to those extending an olive branch.

If you are trying to mend fences, you care. If you are thinking about the offense and how someone hurt you, you care. Hurt says, "I care and I am wounded." You will never live life without the potential or reality of being hurt in interpersonal relationships, especially ones you deeply value. It is just how much maturity you have to see through them and how much love you, and the other party have, to get through difficult times.

# *The Load*

I AM NOT negative. Everyone carries a load; some are lighter than others and others are very heavy. I don't know one person who does not carry a load of some kind. Some events were not asked for, but some they helped accumulate. Loads weigh us down but attitudes determine how far down they will take us.

When we carry a load, we often have a say in how we carry it. Not all the time, but most generally we do have some say. Don't ask yourself if you or your neighbor is carrying a load. Ask yourself how you might carry yours and then... help someone else carry his or hers. Loads are a part of life. How you carry yours will make your life... or break it.

*When the rains come after a dry spell, it speaks of refreshment. Encouragement is like fresh rain. It waters what is dry and offers health to what is living.*

## Rain Encouragement

A word can change an outcome.
An action can restore a weary heart.
Rain can help withered crops and sometimes save the harvest.
Keep on.

Nothing to look forward to?
You don't absolutely know that.
Keep on.

Broken heart and life fractured?
You might be very surprised what is coming to visit you in the days ahead... or even tomorrow.
Keep on.

Loss after loss.
Did you ever stop to think, those losses brought you some gifts?
Keep on.
Yes, keep on.

# *When You Are Down*

EVERY DAY THERE is sorrow in your path or someone else's. Every day there is beauty. How much focus we give one or the other will fill our minds, stir our emotions, and hence, lead our actions. When we are down, it is not easy to get up. It is easy to feel life gave us a raw deal and begrudge the person who got a better one.

I can find people in better places than I am at some level: emotional, physical, spiritual, and mental. I can find people in more challenged places, as well. I can be sad—and I have been sad—because of losing or not having attained in my life something I felt makes a great life.

I can be right about my losses being too much and too costly. However, there are some burdens on others' backs that are just very great in this moment. How will they pay a pressing bill to stay in their home? How will they get medical treatment or if they get it, will it secure them a better and healthier life? How will they find a lover or companion with whom to go through the next years of their life? How will they ever be happy again after so much disappointment and broken dreams?

Sometimes in life, a quote just won't cut it. Thoughts and quotes are there to inspire and challenge our thinking, as do a posting of words, but what if you feel hope has run dry? Let me share a few thoughts—seven of them:

1. **Cry honest tears...** That means release your emotions and let them out, but do it with a search within your heart in honesty about what is troubling you. See, people who are sad, often just feel sad. They have not taken the time to search out their sadness. It's a vague feeling of unease or they may know, but often, sadness becomes their very identity. Stop the world for a minute and ask yourself, "What is really bothering me?" Name it. Identify it.

2. **Go take a walk...** and carry a pencil and paper in your pocket. As you walk, breathe and take in the joys of your senses... your eyes that see, your ears that hear, etc. When you notice anything you have that is good, write it down. Write down any person you love, any food you like, and anything else that is good in your life.

3. **Complete one task...** that needs to be completed and another task that brings you joy in the day. Perhaps you have to do a load of wash or you must cook dinner. Do it. Force yourself, if you must, especially if you have a family or someone depending on you. At times when I felt down, just making dinner seemed monumental, but I forced myself. Keeping a semblance of a routine pulls you out of ruts, just like a tow truck pulls you out of trouble when your car is stuck in the mud. That happened to me... another story for another day! It's a funny one. The one task that brings you joy—never go a day without it. If that is reading a good book, sitting in a hot bath, hitting some balls at the driving range or watching a football/baseball game, do it.

We each have pleasures. Remove them from your days and you take away a part of your life.

4. **Talk to God**, a good friend, or to a stranger... or help someone who will have nothing to give you back other than a smile and thanks. Have those people or events become a regular part of your week. Connection is often as good as medicine and professional therapy. I never let a week pass without good emotional contact—sometimes even daily. That means be involved, not just casually existing around people. When I feel sad for myself and I expect others to come my way, I do two things: 1) I ask God to send me refreshment, and 2) I tell myself to go out and give it.

Oh, the stories I have of mere strangers touching my life and letters in the mail or a call! It's so fun to open your heart to the wind of grace.

5. **Put on music you like...** and let it stir you.

Music is healing. I love some instrumental pieces; they break through my sadness and inspire me again. Music has a way of reaching deeply as it touches and calms you. It seems to create space that helps you come back to solving things.

6. **Write out your thoughts and frustrations**... I often put my angry words on paper; I don't say them to people. Oh, I am known to say some things to people, but my angry and frustrated thoughts go to my journal or writing. Wow! This exercise becomes an eye opener for me a couple of days later. I get to hear myself and see the pulse of my heart; a

heart that never embarrasses me. It is so truthful, how can I punish it for feeling? I do accept my feelings and then I look at what I can do with what I see. Some things, I can't change; that is life. Some things, I can... and now, I do.

I used to be stuck in my anger, which would loop around and around me; not anymore. I choose now to be proactive. I know that going forward in life is risky and uncomfortable, but it is the only way triumph comes. It comes when you go forward... it really does come, in some way or some shape, big or small.

7. **Be an ally to yourself**... No cutting yourself down, no shaming and no blaming; only accepting and owning. Forgiveness must run to us or otherwise we all should just quit. If forgiveness is not operational in great measure in your life, you will be overcome with sadness. We all mess up, sometimes with intention; sometimes not. Learn, change, and begin again. If someone really loves you, you can walk the extra mile; if you love yourself, you will do that. The act of cutting down another represents shame and blame, as a poison you drink, which destroys your thoughts and weakens you.

Nourish your soul. Respect it by accepting what is in your life, what you have contributed to it, what has been given to you, and where you can progress and change. One of the reasons we can't shake depression and sadness is because we cannot accept reality. Reality is the heart place of rational thinking and real acceptance. Reality hurts. Yes, it does... but reality is the place of coping and the place of building or reconstructing the life you were given.

# *I Don't Believe I Will*

I JUST TALKED with a dear friend who lost her mother over a year ago. She wonders if she will ever get over it. I told her, "You won't! Oh, the process of time will make it easier and less strikingly painful, but I don't believe you ever get over someone you deeply loved and treasured."

In fact, the more you deeply love-or are tied to someone, the more I believe you will not get over him or her—nor should you. I do know that time curbs and lessens some of the pain of loss but unless your mind has no memory, there is no "getting over" a deep loss.

This philosophy should free you and help you, not make you mourn! Don't fight a battle that cannot be won. Accept the war it wages within you and make a peace treaty with it. Be so thankful that you could love and experience someone you found full of the delight of life. I may feel sorrow, and want to have the relationship or person in my life longer, but recognize it was a pleasure to have experienced them at all. Their life and love was a gift, which is accompanied by some of the pain or struggle in the relationship. You will never get close to anyone who will not bring you some sadness or struggle, just the very nature of living with another and the sharing of our thoughts sets us up for conflict and differences.

There is so much joy in having someone you cannot get over. I consider it an honor to have had some of those people in my life. Even in heartbreak it shows that you opened yourself to love. How can that ever be failure or final loss? I know it hurts, horribly, to have people and circumstances where you know you won't be able to go forward with them, but life asks this of all of us, at some time, if we are fortunate to have a rich existence filled with experiences. You go forward at first because you have to, but then because you loved them deeply. Your reward, the beauty of that love now becomes a strength you have... to create more love in the world.

## *Chapter Closing*

CAN YOU BELIEVE it? Another summer is almost in the books. I marvel how quickly some things go and how it seems others are a straggler, hanging on. Someone recently told me, "Sometimes, a person loves a book so much, he/she reads it again." I think the past can be like this for us at times... we want to read it and feel it again. This may be from the fond memories of our youth when we went to camp, played baseball in the open lot, or took an awesome trip to the beach or mountains.

Life's repeats come in all shapes and sizes. The past can be desirous to us but we usually can't repeat it. This means to me that I must love today and invite it in, to welcome it. We all close a lot of chapters in our lives. I can remember realizing I had aged when I bought another refrigerator after one did not work. I realized that time all too quickly passed, measured by broken things or things that had served their useful life. The closing of summer is another chapter in my life, and your life. We won't get this same summer again... not in quite the same way.

Find ways to close your life chapters in the best possible manner. Close them without bitterness or hatred or anger— close them with satisfaction. If you find a relationship passed you by, enjoy it for what it was and all it brought you. Don't look back on all the misfortune or loss, at least not too much. Even difficult times have some excitement and beauty as closing chapters. If a dream was dashed or an opportunity missed, can you see it as life stepping in and asking you if your desire is sufficiently real you will try again? Do you not see that what happens to you actually proves you and strengthens you? I believe there are no losers in life, only those who say they will not try again and become quitters.

Closing chapters can be done quietly and with grace. They can also be closed thankfully and with gratitude. They are training places to see where your heart is. Never forsake the growth in the chapters of your life, even the very difficult and tearful ones. Nothing is wasted in a life. Nothing.

# *Here*

AS I PROGRESS in years, I believe more and more in enjoying the present moment. I believe you can only do this when you are awake and real to the moment. That means even the painful ones.

I am learning that if I am sad, I tell myself, "Ok, so I am sad!" I then work from this point of view, to give myself the healing and help I need. I don't fake it and I don't fluff it. I receive my sadness and add a dash of goodness for me in the present moment, knowing it has something positive to bring me. I accept how I feel. I try to never push it away. It is my teacher. It may show me I am off track or just how passionate about something or someone I have become. I receive anger, too, so I might use it properly.

If I come to a place in my life where there is loss, I mourn. My body and mind know it anyway, why would I not agree with them? I walk in harmony with myself when I realize these are threads in my life that I don't need to untie, but work to unite. They are there to do me good, to grow me, and make me savor the length and width of my living

As I experience joy, I feel it **all.** It comes out in my words, my actions, and my gestures. Joy doesn't have to be evaluated, but most assuredly should be celebrated and not tempered by another's dislike or disagreement of how I might find it. I only welcome it, without reducing it or giving it conditions.

The longer I live, the more I feel, and accept my moment-to-moment feelings—good or bad, right or wrong, full or empty, pleasant or sorrowing. I allow myself to see all my emotions working for me and in me. Nothing is against me except when I push experiences aside or fail to embrace the learning in them. Life is for you. Your emotions are for you. Reality is for you. Rich living is found in feeling and believing feelings are here just for you.

## *Depression's Gain*

I AM ACQUAINTED with depression. Depression is not a friend but it is also not necessarily my enemy. I call it my teacher. Years ago it took me down a narrow and treacherous path; it brought me valuable experiences and lessons on my journey. Each of us will suffer some time in depression's wake, different only in degree, and time in its grip. Depression is as old as mankind, and no culture, race, gender or age, has ever gone through life having been totally unaffected by depression.

Still, I am thankful for the lessons depression taught me about my beliefs, my hopes and longings, and who I was in this place called life. Did I get all the answers to my questions? No. Did I need them? No, yet again. In fact, learning to accept the way of life and its story was part of the answer to my inquiry. Some of those answers have come and some continue to arrive throughout my journey, throughout time... and some responses simply may never come. That is ok.

I wanted to hurry out of my period of depression, but you see, I first had to acknowledge the time and direction it took me to get there. A therapist suggested my multi-living places and childhood upbringing and constant change was a possible thread, but how can a child do anything but learn to accept the place he or she was raised in... at least when coming to understand it?

What I learned astonished me and in time healed me, though I have been warned that depression doesn't ever totally heal and episodes can reoccur. They can even be triggered from outside events, such as when someone feels threatened by sorrow and change. That humbles me, but I am ok with that. A particular life is not promised to any of us; we live and move one day at a time—one breath at a time—but we go on, don't we? We go on for love, for life, and for others. I learned many things by asking three questions:

**1. What am I so afraid of?** Fear was so much a part of my life—fear to be careful, fear to do the right thing, fear of what might happen, or fear of what did happen... fear, fear, and more fear. The world looked scary to me as I aged, grew up and pressed on. I experienced change happened sometimes far too quickly as I moved, shifted into my marriage and examined my motivations. None of which really made life easier, but I found coping skills and went along until one day, I knew the beam of depression had actually shined its light on me. Little did I know that it would lighten my path and deliver me through my fears to find hope.

**2.** My second question was, **"Why do you feel so unloved?"** I had a great life, people would tell me, but I didn't connect with my heart or respond to it. I had sanitized my soul by following other's expectations and approval—and that was lonely, even in company. I was often told how to think, how to feel and how to believe and that short-circuited a deeper dive into love and I felt angry and disappointed with myself. You see... love gives freedom to think, believe, and feel. There is room for a rich life when you love and are loved. Love trusts time and finds a way to accept with no need to rush or crush.

**3.** My final question, **"What do you think you are missing?"** Missing things or people makes us feel we were passed by in life—and made more aware we came here to fulfill some of our longings and share our gifts in life. Ask yourself what you need and be honest. Then seek it; work for it, but don't make any particular condition, person, or event **be** your happiness. You will be sorely saddened.

Yes, I answered those questions and it was my depression, which made me look deeply into them. It freed me to live, love, and feel joy. I was made for all that—and just like you—for so much more.

# *Dark Night*

THERE ARE HARD, harsh words when you are in a dark place. Oh, they may be cheerful words, but can still be hard ones. I experienced two very dark nights, each of which in reality lasted far longer than a night. Both times I thought my life was going to end. I actually saw it slip away from me. Now, I am amazed at times, just how much strength the body has to bear some of the upheavals we have in life, and how the mind endures all kinds of pressures. Now, more than then, I am more amazed that new life grows.

You know, when fire ravages an area, it can be devastating, but you know what often happens? The burned debris from grasses and trees becomes fertile and vibrant soil, for new growth. I believe our lives parallel this. I also think nature is much a teacher and mirror of our own life stations. If you feel you are "burning" and the night is dark and long, hold on, you will be rewarded for your struggle. You don't have to know what will grow in your life, just hold on, and trust that it will. If you have been "burned" and you see no life, move along, slowly, planting seeds of hope and steps of peace.

I know, you can't see the end from the middle, but have you ever walked in the dark and turned on a light switch? There was so much around and in front of you that you didn't realize, but it was there, correct? If you have been burned and you are just seeing new life come forth, keep watering and remain expectant in hope. There is life from places you feel death has visited. There is light in places the light has gone out. There is life…

### *Anger is a bad counselor.*

~ French Proverb

# NOTES

# THEME VIII

*I let go so I could hold on.*

~ Carolyn Flinn McCool

## BITTER EMOTIONS

## Me. Angry?

WE SANITIZE A lot of things in life to get along with others and even ourselves. Sometimes, it would just be nice to admit what we think all along, *things are just not right*. We can't, however, in our fear of upsetting someone or altering some event. We are very human, but we like to think we aren't. Many motives show up in what we do and who we are; motives that are often mixed. There is no one with 100 percent pure motives in the field on which we play. Do we quit? No, we learn, gently propose to do better, and recognize the person next to us is growing and as human as we are.

Anger resides not far from any of us. If we are in a place of ease, we may think it is barely near us. But, take one change, one tragic or disastrous event and watch the heat of anger increase. Sure, it may show up behind the gates we build around us, but it will ultimately show up and demand we listen. I once read that depression is often anger not dealt with, which makes it useful to us, if we just give it its proper place. When anger is respected and given a proper vehicle of expression, it is less inclined to run all over people and places.

## The Knapsack

ONCE UPON A time there was a woman who loved to hike and enjoy the out-of-doors. She often traveled long distances and for long periods of time, so she carried a backpack. It was small and more like a knapsack. In it she placed her water and small snacks that went with her as she journeyed. She was comfortably set and so she went.

On one of her hikes she had put a lot of things in her sack. She noticed the pull it had on her as she ascended hills and had a marvelous thought. "I understand the weight of things, like the weight of things in our lives, so I'm going to weigh my backpack down, by filling it with heavy things, and then throw things out as I go forward on my path. This will be like a symbol of removing things that weigh me down."

So she filled her sack with rocks and moved along. It was heavy. It was time to toss a rock out and name it as a weight she had in her life. She thought the first one could be worry. Then the close neighbor, fear, was not long after that. She continued her journey and another rock, called pride, left the sack. Her journey continued and after throwing out many rocks, she noticed her load was not the same; it was lighter. She could move better. She felt less pull from the weight of the sack and it was much easier to press ahead.

A perfect illustration of life for her; she understood you have to be careful what you carry because it can weigh you down and even slow you down. She learned from experience how you travel also determines how you enjoy life.

# The Lesson—When It Doesn't Feel Right

WE SOMETIMES KNOW better, but we don't do better. There are times we can want things so badly, we sell tomorrow for the moment. We betray our own inner gut and instinct and often have to live with some of the bitter tasting consequences of our impulses.

The lesson in bitter taste does not go down well. It is much better to learn life's lessons than to repeat sadness and struggle. For some the lesson may be to not engage in a relationship that doesn't feel right and check first with your heart... for the benefit of your body. For others it may be to speak unkind words behind someone's back, only later to have those words be revealed and the friendship broken. For yet another it may be a lie that you think will protect one person, but when the truth comes out it wreaks havoc on everyone.

Never settle for an uncomfortable feeling and do nothing. You feel poorly and unsettled for a reason—something is amiss and needs correction; needs truth or needs an answer. The lesson can sting for years when you choose against an uncomfortable feeling or instinct; it may cause a breach in a promising relationship, lead someone to never be able to trust you again, or make you feel shame for a very long time. Trust that when you feel badly, the life lesson is to help find a way to help yourself feel good again by honoring your life and someone else's.

# *Life After Guilt*

TOO MANY PEOPLE live their lives in the throes of guilt. I know, I have, and I've spoken with others who do. There is a time to feel guilty. We feel guilty about things we should not, and then are numbed... unable to care about things about which we actually should feel guilty.

Guilt serves to remind us our actions are amiss and we probably need to address what that is. There are times we experience false guilt, which is a general feeling about being guilty without any actual reason to be remorseful. Professionals also address the term as the fear of disapproval in disguise.

Even those feelings need to be addressed and set right. It is good to learn the difference between what is something about which you should feel guilt and when those feelings have no validity, because not knowing could hamper your personal growth and general life.

When you make choices to live with and respect the work of guilt in your life, you can enjoy life more. If you don't learn these concepts, the path you will be unnecessarily hard and confusing. There are absolutely some things one **should** feel poorly about doing. When they occur, or a violation of conscience happens, we are blessed to feel guilt. Guilt should lead us to correction and apology. It can mend relationships as well as allow one to have inner peace. Guilt is not all bad, like it is often portrayed. The right relationship with guilt can actually give you a beautiful life.

# *I Cannot Stay Broken*

I DON'T THINK there are more themes or songs than stories about broken hearts. The experience of a broken heart is universal. It may mean different things to different people. It may happen in different magnitudes, yet, a broken heart is something we all understand. We know that physically the heart does not break, although science teaches us a heart can break in some measure. It sure feels physical when you are going through what you consider a broken heart, doesn't it?

A broken heart can be a gift to you, a gift you won't believe or want, but one that can bring you more than you would get if you felt yours were still whole. Today a friend asked me if I would be in the place I am in, if I would not have struggled through brokenness. I told her, "No, but I can never measure the other side, because I did not experience it!" I can; however, now say the side of a broken heart I did experience was a tremendous gift with growth and joy for me.

The gift of growth and joy didn't happen instantly or willingly. I would have simply passed through every day, but somehow and someway (and I now realize some of the how and way), the tight and wounded bud I had been finally blossomed. I am thankful for what transformed my life. I have the privilege to experience my deepest dreams and desires and I can now see opportunities everywhere I go in my life. What I once thought would be a closed door, is a wide and open one.

If you are any place near a broken heart, I plead with you... do not give up on life and love. Do not talk-down to yourself and punish yourself for your condition or thoughts. Use language to talk "up" to yourself and nourish your soul. Be the one to offer mending and aid to your own heart... first and often. Love, I learned, must come from within me; I must first learn to receive it without condition or criticism. Your heart must be free to give, even at the risk of being wounded again. Not to sound negative, but there is always a possibility of being wounded again... there is no possibility of the joys I now have had I not been willing to put my heart on the line. I am wiser. I learned. I found where my comfort and stability is—and accept it will get tested again. In fact, it already did and guess what? My broken heart came through!

I am richer in soul and mind for a broken heart. That worn and weathered heart is more beautiful and stronger and best of all, loving. Tell me, how did I really lose? Yes, I lost something precious to me but I gained some of life's most beautiful new moments and values. Life is peculiar. How is wholeness found in brokenness? I don't know but I am confident in my knowledge that it is. Continue to take steps forward, and change your perceptions about who you are and what you suffered. Embrace the brokenness as something within to provide you with more, not less of a life. Love is worth all you will give to it, and all you may have suffered for it.

# *Judgment*

I HAVE WATCHED "Little House On The Prairie" which is one of my favorite moral lesson shows from the 70s. There was an accident, which left everyone's goods delayed because the wagon had some malfunction. The incident left the driver pinned under the wagon. Back at Walnut Grove, the destination town, people were most worried about the goods that were not delivered and felt the driver had done something against them. In time, many of the town's people were saying hateful things about the man who was bringing them a product to help them farm. The story... no, the people, got ugly.

A silly show, you may think, but a not so silly result. This kind of ugliness happens when we judge without mercy. We think someone did something and even though we are wrong in our perceptions, we don't care to wait or find out if what we believe is valid. People's reputations are at stake and so is the emotional well-being of many. Bitter words are often spoken, followed by embarrassment when the truth is revealed... truths much different from what you thought they were.

In time the broken wagon and injured driver were found and the townspeople learned the man was not stealing from them, he was pinned under a wagon without aid.

How many times do we need to learn the lesson that judging without just knowledge is dangerous? We can do this to our spouse, a friend or our children. We can assume who ate something in the refrigerator or who took some tool and we can get angry. What is worse is when we learn we were wrong and we fail to apologize. This failure to say we are sorry can break hearts, especially those of children, when repeatedly suggested they are at fault, because we do not take responsibility for our mistakes and failings with them. Don't assume; you might be very wrong. The work to repair judgments is hard and sometimes, what is broken may never be fixed.

## *The Bitter*

WHEN I WAS a child, we loved to eat lemons. They were sour and it was fun to see if we could stand the bitterness. We also liked the smiley lips the fruit would make when cut in a curved shape, and the lemon half placed in our mouth. Bitterness is sour to your life. Oh, it may seem to go down well, at first, but a bad after taste repeats the first sour experience.

Bitterness is expensive; it costs society and our health care system money. It affects people in their homes, in the raising of a family, and the union of man and wife. Bitterness keeps people away from each other; often seen in the breach of families and friends. Sometimes people would rather nurse their grudge than work to remove it. Here are three reasons why I think people like to be bitter:

1. **They get to feel right**. Somehow it just feels good to be so right. When you hold the line at all cost, the action shouts of bitterness.

2. **Pride is easier to wear than humility**. It is harder to squeeze into humility. It requires you give something significant to another person, which is hard for the proud and the stubborn.

3. **It doesn't require the work of reconciliation**. Bridging gaps with people is work. You might have to call someone or write a letter. It might also cost you a sleepless night to gather the courage to work things out with someone.

Bitterness is like stew, though, if you just keep it on the stove and stir it from time to time. It's easy to cook like that. It's the more involved processes of cooking—or managing bitterness—which is more difficult, and like reconciliation... is work.

You can shift yourself from a state of bitterness and change your outlook to an "in-look." Bitterness is sometimes subtle and we often feel we can justify it. I have... I know this place! You think, *someone hurt me and they deserve this nursing place in my heart*. Don't do it; your life is never lived well in bitterness. Don't let it cost you your health, your smile, your love, or your laughter. Bitterness makes beautiful people ugly.

## *There's Enough*

WHEN WE ARE envious, we are saying there is not enough for us and we are not enough in life. Envy will cheat you out of preparing and working toward a useful life. Envy asks to be a short cut to acquire status or being respected. It doesn't want to expend effort or work and can't respect that someone else was recognized. I used to think that envy was for children, but it abounds plenty in adults. It is just spiffed and shined up a little differently.

Don't be a person who wants what someone else has unless you respectfully decide to model their hard work and effort; not chase something you see that is honestly gotten and gained. You will feel so good when you work for what you get and keep your heart in good order while you do it. It is one of the greatest places to live in life!

By the way, there **is** enough in life! Your gifts will make room for you. Develop them at any age and any time; never tell yourself you are done. At 79, Sir John Gurdon won the Nobel Prize in Physics and Medicine, after being told, in a biology class in 1949, he should drop his dreams of being a scientist. Would he have served the world better by being envious that someone had "the gift" and he was not capable of such greatness? No, he kept on. With what are you keeping on? Who has made you quit or told you what you have isn't good enough? Don't let anyone divert the purpose and direction that is born from goodness and desire. You aren't done yet, and you sure don't want to be someone else—or envy someone whom you were not intended to be.

# *Nothing To Argue*

EACH TIME YOU argue with someone, you open or create deep, and possibly painful wounds. Arguing is different than discussion. Discussion keeps a low emotional temperature, whereas arguing raises it. Discussion remains open to listening and correcting misconceptions and error, while arguing closes the doors to compromise and progress. Discussion opens the possibility for love and understanding. Arguing thinks it's getting to the goal, but tears down possible progress in its path, with no desire to rebuild and replant.

Discussion is for the mature. Arguing is for the babe, the infant, or the immature. Discussion lends to life and love. Arguing can lead to death and hate.

Who are you in your conflict? Who do you want to be? Conflict swallows families, parts lovers, and creates the potential for friends to walk away from what they worked hard to build over time. There are no victors in arguments, only remnants of what could have been built from discussion. Here are five things I have learned about arguing:

1. **Solve and resolve** or you risk dissolve.

2. **Talk soul-to-soul**, not face-to-face; heart to heart, not head to head.

3. **Be aware**; you have triggers and weaknesses and you would do well to own your shortcomings. Don't feel compelled to tell the other person what his or hers is.

4. Too angry? **Back off; take a break**.

5. Ask yourself, "**Is this the person I want to be remembered as?**" Angry words, spoken today, may not be easily repaired tomorrow. You can save your tomorrows by a willingness to discuss what is difficult for you today.

# NOTES

Carolyn Flinn McCool

# THEME IX

*Don't let the struggles of life take the most of you and
leave the least of you.*

~ Carolyn Flinn McCool

## FORWARD IS HOPE

# I Hope...

I **HOPE** YOU love with every fiber of your being.

I **hope** you leave no stone unturned as you seek to explore and grow.

I **hope** you get back up after you have fallen down and you come up stronger and with more passion.

I **hope** you remember who has your back and who would walk many miles with you.

I **hope** you laugh with others, and never at them, and you never forget your humanity and beauty.

I **hope** you persevere and never quit unless you do it from courage and conviction and not fear and failure.

I **hope** you embrace the gifts within so the light of your soul will shine brightly.

I **hope** you enjoy the feast of life prepared before you and know that you are a "we."


# The New Day

CHANGE IS A given. Night yields to day. It comes; it is scheduled by nature and we know it. We often don't know when change comes for us, though. We often don't even want it. What has happened has happened. Mom always told me, "You can't rewrite your memories in how they happened."

You can rethink them, but what happened, happened—and time will never change that.

Ouch! Does that suggestion hurt? Possibly, but it can also let you know you can gather strength from your memories. You are more courageous **in** them... you are wiser **for** them... and you are walking **from** them. Let the new day come and be thankful for what it gave... even if it brought a tear—even if it set you back. You get something for your troubles; use them for something good. God declares things are for us and life is for us, and I am all for trusting the kind of change that will create more wonder and beauty in life.

# *Be Done!*

BE DONE WITH what you can't fix. Be done, if you have given the effort to put matters right. I don't believe we are called to punish ourselves into oblivion. I don't even believe God would do that to us, though there were times in my life I didn't think so kindly of Him.

Be done with the constant need to worry about every mistake you have made, who is angry with you or who doesn't think well of you.

Be done, if you had a change of heart, and seek to be a peacemaker. If you don't let go and move ahead, you might affect your future and hurt other people and ultimately... yourself.

Sometimes, we get the idea that we have to pay—forever—for things we may or may not have done. I think that is a very tall judgment and one where we are playing God. Though I don't think we should take our mistakes and sins lightly, I do feel we have to be careful lest we open a place within ourselves to condemn and be unforgiving.

Would you not give reprieve to someone who came to you for pardon and apology, and with a changed heart? Would you? Give that to yourself. Some of our minds are so heavily written in the pain of our past, we pronounce sentence without a trial. Learn of mercy; learn to live mercy.

## *I Let Go, To Hold On*

**As I watch fall's leaves drop,**

I ask myself the question...

What or who is it I must let go?

I have learned there is always something I carry that has need of release.

**Is it:**

An attitude that inflicts me;

A habit that pulls me inward or downward;

Or is it something or someone that must fall just like autumn's leaves?

Clutching fists cannot make room for the next season's coming delights.

**Time comes. Change asks. Life goes forward.**

> Behind me is nothing that steers my life to life, unless it is love

**Fear is a waster of days**

> A forgetter of goodness and
>
> A forfeiter of present happiness

**I let go,**

> So I can hold onto what is coming for me.

# *Determined*

NEVER GIVE UP ON your dreams, especially when you strive to grow. Hard work is purposeful work. Remember that a child never begins by walking... he or she begins by crawling. He or she begins by first being a child and growing. You get places when you honor the process and the steps to get there. Determination gives you something quitting won't.

# *Imagine*

**IMAGINE...**

John Lennon sang it, a New York sidewalk proclaims it, entrepreneurs think it, and you will soar with it! The possibilities and joy of "Imagine" are everywhere. They are by your side, near your heart, in your head, and waiting to be written in your soul!

**Just imagine...**

the telephone to someone on the Mayflower,

the light switch to pioneers in vast traveled lands, or

a plane ride for Leonardo DaVinci!

Everyone one of these scenarios was initially filled with the idea of "Imagine," but with unrealized imaginations, many were filled with the thought, *not possible.* Look today at what imagination does and brings!

Throughout your life and mine... we face challenges every day:

**Some people are challenged to even find breath this morning;**

**Others face a severe disappointment;**

**Still others will only imagine what their labors and thinking prowess can bring.**

Imagining is your best self thinking, *I will not settle for what I am afraid I cannot do or whatever reason and people point to and say is not in me. I will quest. I will open the door. I will reason. I will turn over that stone because I know something good comes from the place of imagining.*

Release the ropes

Lift the sails

Ride the winds

Soar to new heights

Imagine

# NOTES

# THEME X

*The chance you won't get is the one you won't take. Go. Do. Be there.*

~ Carolyn Flinn McCool

## DARING AND DOING COURAGE

# *Jump*

THERE ARE TIMES we must jump. We may have the choice to run or turn in a different direction, but sometimes, the best or most reasonable choice is to jump. Today I watched a young bikini-clad child jump into the arms of her mother as she went off the diving board. Guess what? The young sport did it again and again. She did it with cheer, chatter, and delight. Her mother, repeatedly, was there for each jump. She was happy to assist her young one, and the smile of approval and delight was on the mother's face, too.

It brought back sweet memories of when my kids jumped off the diving board, but what touched me was the trust shared between the two of them, mother and daughter. The little girl could jump with abandon because she knew someone would have arms to catch her. This thought made me think of God and grace. *Do I know the arms I can jump into that will catch me, hold me, and help me as I go all out to life?*

We do a lot of "jumping" in life. We find those who will support us and those we can count on. From a new venture that holds promise, yet uncertainty... to a new relationship that holds our hopes of love... to living and growing old. It makes the jumping much easier when you have arms to catch you, doesn't it? You won't go under, though you may have a rough landing.

## *The Gift To Go On*

ONCE UPON A time there lived a girl who thought everything had to be **right and just so** in order to be happy. So, she tried and tried to make others happy. She would sacrifice her happiness or inconvenience herself so others would find theirs, and learned in time this particular strategy was an exercise in futility. It frequently never made others happy and just as often didn't help her cause. In fact, she was nothing more than profoundly sad.

Then one day, when something very distressing happened, she realized she had it all wrong! It was only from the wellspring of her joy could she create and be happy. When her joy spilled over it might **touch** someone but it was most certainly not her **job** to create their happiness. Other people had to receive and find joy from their well, too.

She learned that her joy was hers... she was responsible for it she was to be honest with it, and she was to use it to create her life, kindly and with grace. It wasn't long after that she found her well rising. It was true water, fresh water, and water that satisfied... all because she learned to trust her joy and realize it was good enough. It had been good enough all along.

# We Are Asked

LIFE ASKS A tremendous amount of us. We are asked to start in a helpless and needy state to grow and mature, and many times, we leave in the same helpless or needy state.

> **Try looking at your parent in diapers. Yes, the one who protected you and led you along to be settled and secure in life; how has their state changed and how will it impact you?**

> **Try looking at your future, even if it is broken and fragmented by a past illness or accident, and discover how you can continue on... cheerfully.**

> **Try looking at family conflict that tosses you out of the gatherings or casts light on you that you are someone you are not, and embrace the reality you still move forward.**

Yes, life does a lot of us—and maybe it has of you.

Some of the most courageous people I know were born in the trial... in the fire. An easy life does not temper the soul, but a difficult one may. Life can be difficult, but I reason that all of our lives have difficulty, to some extent and degree, while others are at best very challenging. It is courage that is often the ingredient that will put your feet to the floor... you will go on.

It is your courage that says, "I am not done yet. There is something in the "forward" and I will not let the "backward" own me. There is courage in reality and acceptance, not in denial or glibness about my station in life. Reality is the most efficient place in which to make a life. It is said, "Courage doesn't roar," but it sure does make a strong movement in the soul, and if I could give volume to movement, it would be loud!

## *One Person*

EVERY ONE OF us is one person. Not a brilliant observation, but follow me. However, you are part of someone else and they a part of you.

**The very baby that needed your nourishment in the womb now needs your continued care today.**

**The older person who comes into your business has little, but you are the sunshine to their day, as they are to yours, when you exchange greetings.**

**An angry teen, who didn't like your rules or discipline, needs your love and acceptance today.**

**The person who is driving slowly in your lane, could use a sweet name or hello when you pass them, rather than a cross word or thought.**

**The spouse or friend who struggles with work and direction is one person you can reach... or you can lovingly try.**

Every day I see how one person or one response can change the tone of a conversation or outcome of it. I also know how one poor tone or response can hurt... not only in the moment, but for many tomorrows. It is not someone else who will feed your baby, talk to the older person at the store, hug an angry teen, smile at a passerby in the car beside you, or listen to a struggling spouse or friend. It is you and me, doing what one person does... look, care, help, and love. One person who cares for another is a powerful number. Wonderful things happen with one person.

## *Today Is My Day*

BELIEVE IN THE value of today. Too many times it is easy to think tomorrow will be the day to diet, live, or attack a problem. Tomorrow is a beautiful and opportunistic day, but it is a day that is not a reality; you cannot do tomorrow today!

The California State University, in Chico, boasts the slogan, "Today Decides Tomorrow." Every time I see this slogan I feel encouraged. Really, is life not made up of using your today well? Tomorrow remains a hope and a wish. Today is an arrival and a workroom. Love your todays and fix your heart on using today for what it is, a promise received and a present focus.

Passing on the possibilities of today often speaks of fear and indecision. There are times it is prudent to wait and proceed with caution, but to always live the slant and supply of your life based on tomorrow is a waste of today's possibilities!

## *Not Too Late*

SO YOU MADE a mistake! You can't change it. It is done. You lost the love you thought should be your life. You suffered financial loss or physical illness. You didn't win the job promotion or win the match in your high school playoff game. It didn't happen to you quite like you wanted it to, like you thought it would, should or could. But I imagine...

You had someone looking out for you at some time in your life. You still can hear their words, shed tears of gratitude and express difficult emotions. Perhaps you received a new bike for your birthday that you loved and cherished when you were a child. You played outside with the neighborhood kids and even walked with some of them to school. You bought your first car and you took great care of it with the money you made at your first job. You had someone to be with on Thanksgiving, or your cat recently curled up on your lap. Someone phoned you to tell you 'hi' and tell you they were thinking about you. Someone told you they loved you.

If you look more deeply, you must realize just how full your life is. One day you will look back and realize it was more than you imagined, even as you believed you needed more. One day, you will realize and firmly implant in your mind, *today is enough, yesterday was full of gifts, even in the hard times, and tomorrow is still an unopened present.* Don't waste your time comparing your life, your family, your finances, your abilities, your heart or your best to anyone. We often do, but why? How does it make us more fit to live and enjoy life? Love what is yours and who is near and dear to you. As a woman told me last year while I was shopping in another town, "Love that tree. Love breath. Love that child. Love life. Love everything."

# That's What Life Is For

IT WAS A cold and rainy day.

She sat down, sitting by the window, looking out, but looking inward realized she was low in spirit. She had no one now, or at least, so she thought, even in the friends and family who were still with her.

"My special rose is gone—who will love me like that, again?" she whispered to herself, as her head fell downward. She traveled back in memory to all the smiles and hugs over time, time when love was spoken and made with her rose. "Oh, it was good, so very good and I didn't know it, like I know it now," she exclaimed. "I didn't realize the moment was one of giving... even those moments that weren't exactly as I wanted. I see them now as precious; I now realize they were for me, for someone, and for love."

..."Yes, those piles of dishes after a meal, that said there was love and company here. Yes, the ever-present abundant amount of wash and tasks that needed to get done, that spoke of having someone I could give my care. Yes, that interruption to ask a question when I was busy, that spoke of someone needing me. Yes, that stormy weather that would bring neighbors out to help others in need, that said we are all in this together. Yes, oh yes, there were so many gifts of love, and I just didn't see them at the time, when you were here."

As her eyes lifted up and looked outside, she noticed a clearing in the dark clouds that were filled with rain, A hint of radiant color broke through to reveal a beautifully arched rainbow. The sun peered behind the broken clouds and the rain stopped. Her heart was beating wildly and it was full, again, even in her loved one's absence. Her low was lifted.

All her thoughts that had churned from the painful memory of her loss, reminded her of the gain; she smiled and thoughts resounded in her innermost soul, *I have today, though I no longer have yesterday. What gifts might I be overlooking today that I will say I had yesterday? I will not let today's joys, or possibilities for joy, escape me, even if they come in ways I don't understand them, and I will be thankful for the treasure of yesterday... because enjoying others and life—that's what love is for.*

## *Question Quitting*

HOW MANY TIMES were you so close, but you didn't know it? How many times have you let a dream go because you wouldn't see it through? Every day we build something, with the resources we have, to take us somewhere. Many of the building materials we use to construct come from the resources of our belief systems and abilities. Every time we don't give up and stay the course in any endeavor, we build confidence and strength. We do not know all outcomes and this is as it should be... but we do know much of what we can put into building our lives.

Build a today with faith, with hope, with love, with promise, with conviction, with determination, and with desire.

If you quit, you won't see it. Your breakthrough is coming; it may even be today.

## *Not Afraid To Tell You*

SOMETIMES WE DON'T tell the people who are in our lives how very much they mean to us, and someday we may not be able to let them know. None of us know how many days we will share together. Life moves along quickly.

There are irritations and rifts that create misunderstandings, along with the every day pressures that disconnect us from the people around us who we deeply value. Walls are built, which keep hearts from other hearts. But people are too important and their well-being needs tending. Someone needs a good word from you, or perhaps you need a good word from someone you treasure.

## *A Friend Called Courage*

COURAGE IS FOR cowards. Much of the time that is who courage is for! My father was a pilot. I flew a fair amount of times in my life, but as I aged, I became more afraid to fly and that fear flowed into other things I considered. Youthful ignorance gave way to adult calculation and fear. With it, fear took much of the joy from my life. I calculated before I did anything; I came to belief that was a safe way to live.

One day I told dad I was afraid to fly, though I always got on a plane, and he proceeded to tell me why I should not be afraid. As we talked he looked at me and said, "Babe, you have more courage than you believe. Look at you, you are afraid but you do it anyway." Dad touched my life and heart. I get it now as I think back on that conversation. Courage is for me, the one who was afraid, yet with that fear was an invitation to come to life and trust it, to respectfully enter it, with a full heart.

You see, living without courage robs you at every level in life. It hurts your marriage. It hurts your friendships. It hurts your ability to work and especially, it hurts your potential pleasures. You can't or won't have fun if you can't walk with courage. I am not willing to give my life away to constant fear or the lack of courage. Sometimes it takes a crisis to make us change and that happened to me, along with loving parental prodding.

So much of what scares us is only in our imagination or can I boldly say, "Only in my imagination!" There are real risks to living every day but why would I want to make more of them? I want to die living, not die being dead already. Go! Do what your heart wants and longs to do. You will be so glad you found courage and made it your friend.

## *The Higher Road*

HOW MANY PEOPLE are a friend to themselves? Think about it. Are you the friend to yourself you are to others:

understanding, forgiving, respectful, and hopeful? You are the friend you need in life. You can't go in life alone, without yourself, but there are many people who do try it alone... and without their own friendship. How say you?

Anytime you give up on yourself, take the cheap or cheating way, speak cutting and condemning thoughts to your spirit or lower your standards and give yourself away to anyone who does not value your soul... you walk without the friend you need at your side.

The higher road is where you walk with yourself as a friend, you work with yourself as a companion, and you climb with yourself as receiver of forgiveness and a seeker of growth. The higher road may have its struggles, but it will never leave you out in the rain or in low places. It's a place of daring and doing. It's a place of going on, not going alone.

## *The Nest Of Life*

HAVE YOU EVER taken the time to look at a bird's nest? Strings, straw, threads, and things that appear like trash often become part of a bird's home. The human home is where babies are rocked, feed, and supported as well. Purpose and life live here. So similar to a nest is the weaving of your own life. You take a string of joy here, a straw of sadness there, some threads of love, and some things you may feel you don't want or need in life that you may even call trash, but you use them to build your home.

Sometimes, we are like the bird that uses whatever resources it can find at the time, to build and live. Yesterday I saw a nest; it had Christmas tinsel built in it and I thought, *how resourceful was the little bird who built this nest; did it complain about what life handed down?*

We don't always get to pick every thread in our "nest." There are strings we will have to take in order to make them useful to us. What a beautiful nest this bird built; strong, steady and complete. I so believe we are asked to take our strings, straw, thread, and trash and believe we can make something beautiful. I believe we can.

## The Best Of Today

I WILL MAKE the best use of this day; some days will find me in a better frame and I will do better. I have choices, even if I feel they are limited. I will act out of a respect for my heart and the very life I am given.

I don't know about tomorrow, and I don't have to. Therefore, for today the pen writes the story and I have just to remember I don't walk alone, for others have taken similar paths. I can learn from them. I can appreciate them. I can value their story. I will not waste what I know. I will use the best of me and no one can take that from me.

# NOTES

Carolyn Flinn McCool

# THEME XI

*Friendship lights the soul of those blessed by its reach.*

~ Carolyn Flinn McCool

## FRIENDSHIP AND KINDNESS

## *Milestones*

THEY ARE EVERYWHERE in life. Putting your child on the school bus is a milestone. Parents everywhere have done it. You get your first job out of college. You marry. You settle in your first house. You lose a parent. You retire. Milestones are joys. Milestones are sorrows. When it was empty nest time in my house, I thought I would die. It was the ending of one chapter I dearly loved and the opening of another I quite feared. We all made it through, though it was rough sailing at times.

Be tender with your milestones and the process of reaching them. Remember, they teach you to value life and what you have, as you live. Milestones are seasonal reminders that all life changes, people change, and time goes on. You must find ways to go on with them.

"What I regret most in my life are failures of kindness," said George Saunders in a 2013 commencement speech at Syracuse University. Kindness is memorable. It's a record to play again and again. We often have regrets of what we **have** or **haven't** done. The milestones of regret often focus on us; kindness focuses on others without excluding us in its joy.

Milestones of kind words help change relationships. A simple kindness can open a new future; inspire a new beginning. Kindness is a game-changer. What good is anything received if it required an act of unkindness to obtain?

Kindness involves life and the heart. It will always be substance over style.

# *A Kind Word*

WHEN I WAS newly married, a man told me the best advice for marriage was to "Be kind." At the age of 22, I thought that was a bit simplistic and narrow. I mean, why tell a newly married person to be kind, they are generally over the moon with their newly joined partner. I learned shortly afterward and beyond, he was so right.

Being kind is about the greatest action in which you will ever engage... for yourself and someone else. Sometimes your kindness is needed, as though the person was starving for it! Sometimes you will need that kindness... at a time it will help lift and hold you. Being kind has no expiration dates and is timely, all the time.

I once sat in an Internet cafe and the man next to me came to sit down. He was carrying a beautiful piece of carrot cake that caught my eye. I commented, "That looks so good!" He held it up to me and offered me some. Now, that gesture was very kind of him; however, he was sitting with two other women and we all started to talk... and continued to talk. It was nice. It was kind. All those things transpired because of someone being kind.

What or who in your life needs your kindness? I know there is someone, near or far. Maybe some child needs your understanding instead of your correction; perhaps your spouse needs a bit of encouragement instead of your frustration and disappointment.

Like a soft blanket, kindness covers life well. How well have your covered your world? Like the rest of the world, I am human and can always do better. Sometimes a lot in life rides on your kindness... or my own. Would you not quickly fix your tire if it were flat? What about the things in your life that need a lift or some air? Kindness lifts them and life rides well.

## *Always My Friend*

THERE ARE MANY things one needs in life but nothing quite so precious as a friend. You could have all the money in the world, look at the most spectacular views, and eat the most exotic cuisine, but it would be nothing compared to sharing joy and sorrow with a friend. Friendship is love that remains and grows.

Self-love and respect is so vital and necessary, yet the truth remains... we can't do everything for ourselves. We need others to come through for us, to sharpen and inspire us, and to create a world where we are safe enough to learn the ways of love. In friendship we grow in places that would be impossible without it.

Friendship is food that sustains and refuels you whether the way is hard or joyful. The companionship of a friend helps you know strength and feel laughter! Friendship must never be one sided, though, or you would question its merit. You don't chase friends so they will care about you; friendship is the road you travel, together, in all seasons and storms life brings you. You can be separated, sometimes, but you will find each other and your love will only have grown deeper—if that friend is really a friend.

Yes, walk beside me, so we share that we are equals, that your vision and love is mine, as it is yours, that we cross the finish line, together, because we were in this all the way... always.

## *Travel With Love and Joy*

PLEASE, I KNOW they tell you to not leave home without your American Express card, but I ask you to not leave home without love. Culture love and grow it—inside first—so you can take it everywhere with you. There is never too much love in the world and yours adds to the best of life. I love seeing the fire of hope and joy in others. It is pretty cool to watch hearts enlarge and dreams blossom. Oh! Never put out the fire of your dreams, no matter how old or lost you may be or feel.

Here's a little wish for you... just so you keep on and to remind you love is like a baton to pass on to other travelers:

May you have...

**Enough challenges to make you climb higher but not too many obstacles to discourage you.**

**Enough wisdom to know you are valuable and so is everyone you meet on your journey.**

**Enough strength to find your calling, enough grace to carry it through, and enough heart to reach out to others in their places of need.**

**Enough success to sustain and refresh you, but not so much to cause you to forget your humanity, or be proud of that success.**

**Enough hope to keep going and to be a friend to yourself when you feel disappointed with life.**

**Enough love to do all your work with cheer and purpose and plenty of forgiveness for those who wound and do not know what they are doing ... and even then will need immense forgiveness for their own hurts.**

May you know you are enough, because you are here, at this moment in time, and because you matter to the moment and another person—and that is enough; you are enough.

## *Friend For The Distance*

A FRIEND WILL never mercilessly judge your life, especially if they love you. They may not see events as you do, but they usually try. Friends offer you another look at things, to understand a little more, and continue to walk with you. A friend has his or her own journey. You cannot take it; you have your own journey. You alone must make your journey, but good friends often walk those journeys alongside each other. That is what a friend does... walks beside you.

Friendship drives you to see more of someone, but not love them less; to forgive, to talk, to care, and to refrain from bitter judgment and unkindness. We don't do this one hundred percent of the time, but real friends do the work to get things right and make them better... Jealousy, judging, and unhappiness with someone over how they deal with a situation is not "friendly."

Yes, a friend can wound you, but both you and that friend will find a way to love through the pain. That is simply what loving friendship does: it finds a way: one to the other. Those who do not find a way to us simply do not love us in true friendship. They may have respect in care or concern for us, as a person, but they do not have the deep well of friendship that goes the distance. Friendship gets to your heart and keeps it.

## *You Surprised Me*

WE ALL GET down sometimes. We even get down when we seek to be strong and find ways to be empowered and positive in life. We may have an issue that came up or a problem we must struggle and deal with. We may not let anyone else know of our struggles, but we know. We may come across as pleasant and happy to others, yet we choose not share the fact we are not on top of the world, so they can pass us by and never know. There are times we can think others have it all together or it looks like their life is the life we would want.

Don't envy another life, another person, or another path. You don't have a clue what their life really looks like. You may be surprised—your life may be the life they want.

Recently I sat next to a young woman on a flight. She was so energetic and full of life that she encouraged me. She was very excited to share her life, as she was marrying soon. We talked the whole two-hour flight. Then as we were landing, she turned to me and said, "I want to thank you for talking to me, I was really feeling down when I got on this flight, and I feel so much more encouraged now. I am really glad I got to sit next to you."

I was almost speechless. Here, this beautiful, happy young girl, who could have been my daughter, was telling me about how much she loved her work and upcoming life-to-be, and then she told me she had been feeling down. I didn't expect those words to come from her mouth, "I have been feeling down." Sometimes we have days or periods of time in our life when we feel blah or we just feel less. It's ok. It's human. It's how life is some days. Sometimes we need nothing more than a kind ear. Sometimes we just need rest. Sometimes we need a new direction. Sometimes we just need time. Sometimes we need nothing other than the will to come back again to face life.

## *How to Apologize*

OVER THE YEARS I have read countless articles on the "apology." You know, I wanted to make sure I gave a proper one and I certainly wanted someone to do the same for me. Today, I feel very different about an apology. It would be nice if someone felt exactly like I did and would want to cover each step to say they are sorry, but I have learned we all don't read or walk the same steps. I learned that I might hinder a much-wanted reconnection by demanding an apology in a way that I feel it should be scripted. I know steps are good principles to follow, but I have found that sometimes people, especially men, apologize in a different way.

Men often feel very sorry about hurting or causing a woman conflict, but they don't always think or believe they can mend it to a woman's satisfaction, so they go on feeling they have apologized... often unclear whether it was to her satisfaction and they just hope she will overlook the matter.

My mom always tells me that men are very tender and much more so than we are aware. I find that is true, as I grow in age and wisdom. Sometimes they just want to begin again after a difficulty, and not have the matter rubbed in their face, while I think women want to have the parameters of an apology set, to believe it is real and you mean it. Now, this is a generalization and it doesn't follow all gender, but I have seen it in operation.

When we have people that don't apologize as we want them to, we tend to stifle the return of connection, until we think they have satisfied us. I think this is terrible for two reasons:

**One, it makes you get in the "conditional" side of accepting others. People don't progress very well when they have to meet conditions. You never can be certain you have met someone's condition when you still have some conditions hanging over you.**

**Two, love and respect must be the change in any relationship problem. If you see that progressing, do you really need a verbal or written apology? I think someone who changes or attempts to do so, shows by his or her actions, they are apologizing. Why hang them out to dry for a technical formality? To me, that is just the voice of pride asking to be an equalizer.**

Relationships are not equalizers. There are times someone will need to give more than you and vice versa. Watch that you don't fall in the trap of meeting someone half way. Love, real and honest love, meets another where there can be communion and fellowship again. Love is not so concerned that you get your way, as it is that you found each other again.

Relationships are precious. Apologies are necessary in even the best of them. Don't make an apology have to be so exact or extracting. Sometimes, just listen to someone's heart in a good and loving light. You will be surprised how unconditional affection brings out connection.

## *Friends Are For Keeping*

WHAT WOULD YOUR life be like without a friend? Lonely and missing something, I would say. I am all for being your own best friend, and I enjoy my company and friendship, but I sure do love my friends! I hope you have an especially close friend or two. Someone you can call or text and know they will be there... maybe not always in body but certainly in soul. Within a friendship, you don't demand or expect, but you freely offer yourself and live graciously wherever that offering lands. You temper everything you share with the love and loyalty you have, so you can bend when there are faults and failings.

I am so tired of things I read that act like love makes no mistakes. Well, maybe love does not, but people do! You find good things in relationships when you go the distance with others. No one can tell me they love anyone with whom they have not gone the distance—and sometimes that is a far distance. I love those people, even if and when they have hurt me. I am no different from you... I have been hurt and I have caused hurt. Life is just not so "neat and tidy" even with good actions and intent, never mind how hard it can be with bad actions or intent.

Today I wrote this to a friend, when I shared a neat post from a writer, I thought it would challenge and encourage her. This is what followed: "I love you and I am unafraid to tell you the truth—and I believe you are unafraid to hear it—and that is why I think you are my friend." Now I know there are more reasons to friendship, but realize one great gift of friendship is being true and learning to be truer. We give those we care about chances and we should. Yes, there are times when rules do not apply because life is not "neat and tidy." However, it is so great when we have love and friends and our shared understanding of love and friendship is mutually understood.

# *You've Got A Friend*

All it takes is a smile and being interested. I once spoke with someone and revealed something about myself and I playfully remarked, "Oh, I just told you something you didn't know." I then turned to them and said, "Since I told you one thing about me that you didn't know, what is one thing I don't know about you?" I was surprised how honest the person was. He said to me, "I carry around the past and it is hard to let it go." I could see the sadness in his face.

He explained to me he had a divorce early in his life and it still breaks his heart because he loved the other person and did not want to separate.

We are tender people, aren't we? Now, we may not always show that to one another, but I think it is a safe bet to say we walk among many tender hearts. It's an opportunity to encourage and lift. It's a chance to bring positive out of the negative or help out of the difficult.

You know, the relationship I have with this new person forever changed. I will strive to take extra good care of that heart. I think that is what connection and honesty does for us, don't you think? It makes us realize how we are more alike than we are different in our needs and hopes.

# *What You Came For*

LOVE YOUR FRIENDS and family and those who you want to love you—and those who need a loving hand. Don't wait for them to offer you a kind word or love you in the way you want, just be love and show it! You cannot know the full heart from which someone is coming from, and thinking the worst of someone offers no benefits to either person. Even if love is one sided, there are benefits and it opens the possibility of future connection and hope... while it grows grace in your own heart.

Cutting off people because they do not please us is like kicking a door and expecting it not to hurt. We must come to learn that those who hurt us sometimes care for us the most, but are struggling with their own insecurities and issues. Our friendships are the playgrounds for lessons where we can learn how to love. You do not have to accept their hurt as proper behavior and you can lovingly call it out, but do what love came down for—to be a difference and make one!

# NOTES

Carolyn Flinn McCool

_____

_____

_____

_____

_____

_____

_____

_____

_____

_____

_____

_____

_____

_____

_____

# THEME XII

*The Wisdom of When… to let something go or continue to stay*
*The Wisdom of Now… love on your path*

~ Carolyn Flinn McCool

## WAITING WIDSOM

## *Every Day Counts*

THERE **IS A** song I remember that contained the lyrics, "Everyone's working for the weekend." It sounded great because I know when Friday rolls around, it's the weekend and that often means fun to people. I understand why Friday can be loved, but how is Monday a bad or sad day, as it is so frequently expressed? I even remember the Carpenters sang the song, "Rainy Days and Mondays Get Me Down."

I know we pay attention to days and we anticipate events and things we do, so weekends are often filled with activities, and we long for the people we will see. That is awesome and life is joyously lived but there is only **one** Friday and six other days. It is also only five o'clock p.m. one time in the day. Thinking to get to Friday or get to a certain time of the day is scarcity thinking. You think you don't have enough good stuff in the rest of the day or week.

Each day you and I have is a gift... a gift we will never experience in the same way again. Now I know, we are sometimes thankful we never will get a certain day again. I know I am. I have had some days I would pay to forget, but life does not work that way, so I will not. When we wish to be somewhere we are not, we waste the day or some of it.

We waste it in worry or thinking we haven't got it good, or worse to me, we think only what is coming is better. Better is right before you. Better is working with what you have and doing something to change things if need be. Better is being so glad you have who and what you have right now, even though there may be situations you wish were improved or nicer. Better is here—not there. Better is now. You don't ever know if you will get Friday. I know people who did not get that much-awaited Friday. Take care of your todays; they are and will remain the best and better days.

## *Where It is Safe*

WHEN WILL WE learn, and how long will it take for us, to realize that risk is what makes our lives full and how we learn? Safety and caution, from life, is mostly an illusion and a fallacy.

You are safest when you know your heart and trust it. You are safest when you tie yourself to hope and leap. You are safest when you believe the good things in life are not just for others but for you, too!

## *Savoring What Is Before You*

I STOP FOR unicorns!

Have you ever seen those signs on the back of a car that names something **they** stop for? Well, I guess I would stop for a unicorn, but I must tell you the truth... I never have seen one, so I have never stopped, but I have stopped for plenty of other reasons.

Who or what are you stopping for? Who is stopping for you? I remember when the kids were very young and their demands were very high. They loved to go somewhere to look at toys and kid stuff. Moms and dads can only take so much kid stuff (well, at least this mom), but I often knew that my respect for what they loved was teaching them their needs were important, too. Our trip to a nearby mall often ended up being a fun time to see all the nifty toys, and it was a great break for a winter day. The kids were in their element and they loved it. I learned that we each have things that get us excited in life—and many times it is not the same thing that excites me—but you tie your heart with others when you "love what they love."

When you slow down and listen to what excites your spouse, friend or child, you can learn things and appreciate them, too. Even today, my husband talked my ear off about something very important to him, which I had little clue about, but I engaged and listened. Slowing down for others often brings a smile to their face and a skip to their step. People go better in life when you have stopped for them.

So, slow down! Have you seen the colors of the flowers along the path you walked today? Can you remember how many traffics lights it is from your house to the grocery store? Do you remember if the last person who walked by you was young or old? Did you smile at someone today on your path who you will never see again and laugh wildly with someone you will? We can think that hurrying gives us more life but slowing down will give us a more meaningful one (I stopped for this sunrise).

There are just some things in life that are so special. They are so special because those things are uniquely your—and mine. They are the marks we leave on hearts, and others leave on ours. They may also be "time sensitive", in that they only last for a short period of time. Every once in a while, though, we get a chance to go back to that time, which often takes us back in heart, but many times it is the wisdom of now which tells us "This is the time, savor it."

## *There Is Something About Ordinary*

I LOVE THE ordinary. There is great blessing in the every day... the routine, and the "count on" things and people of life. Through the ups and downs and the successes and failures, there really is beauty all around us. Today is "touch overload" day for me. I was going to say "Touchdown" but it really was a "Touchup" in that my soul was lifted up.

I marvel at what one soul to one soul does. The love between a husband and a wife, the love between a mother/father and child, the compassion of one person to the next, and a friend that is a friend forever—well, they just amaze me. It's always in our power to bless and love, and that is even with people we struggle with, don't like or who have hurt us. You won't be the same for the giving; neither will those you love and bless.

Oh, yes, tears are falling right now. When I see the beauty of a woman I have never physically met, but our writing collided our lives. She who had cancer, who has shared her story with me, who would send me a tape of her singing, her gift and joy, I weep. When someone sends a letter to tell you what amazing kids you have, and you know they have seen your life on display over the years, and they just want to tell you... that is kind; that is the beauty and touch of the ordinary. It meets you where you live.

Then a beautiful woman I wrote with on a page recently lost her precious animal and wrote a tribute that so touched me. We have an aging and failing animal and part of the joy of life is still living it, even in that sorrow. So today found me with a watchful eye, as I took him outside, while he hobbled to his favorite past outdoors spot where he cannot be left unattended.

Touched. We are all so blessed to be touched and then— to touch. I even posted something on a page and a lovely friend made a beautiful comment that made me smile, as if the story wasn't enough touching, there was more.

Keep your heart open to life. You will get hurt. You will get used. You will get misunderstood, but that is only a small cost of the great joy you will get for being available and loving.

## *Giving Trust*

TRUST... LIFE IS built on trust. Oh, how horrible a fall when trust has been broken. Have you ever been on either side—the one breaking trust or the one where it has been broken? It's pretty painful, isn't it?

There is peace in hearts when trust is part of the relationship. There is respect to and from a heart when trust is present. Trust breeds trust, and it breeds the responsibility to keep it. Distrust breeds more distrust, and it has the possibility of separating people, forever.

Once trust is broken, it takes time to mend i—and sometimes, that mending may be long, or even sadly, may not be possible. We must be careful to whom we give our trust, but to never trust is quite possibly just as dangerous a way to live.

## *Something Grows In A Waiting Heart*

SOMETIMES THINGS ARE covered from our view. They are right there, but we don't see them. It might be only for a short time, and then what was always there, is revealed. Other times, the covering lingers, and we don't see what is really near us.

We can think something we want or need is far from us, or maybe won't appear, but really, it is not true. It just may not be time for things; things just may not be "ready" to be

166

revealed. Sometimes it is just not the time for us to receive them. We may see just a hint of what is, but want more, and if we unwilling to wait, we stress and frustrate ourselves, for what will come—in its own time.

When we are willing to wait and enjoy the waiting, by growing to understand life's way, things happen and views come to us, even if only gradually. The heart is strengthened and stretched through our purposeful waiting. Sometimes we find peace before we find the pieces we are looking for. In the viewing, we can then stand in appreciation and awe of what we are witnessing... what was really always there.

## *Time Explained*

LIFE IS PECULIAR. I mean, you just can't always link A with B or see the reason and rhyme in matters. As a writer, I find this so true. There are things I write that I think are "winner-winner chicken dinner" and no one seems to care. Though a writer never really knows who cares.

I once received a letter, after fifteen years of it being sent, from someone who had found my letter in her attic. She used it to tell me how much I had helped her life. I didn't know that for fifteen years. I mean, like... really know that. So I have learned to not expect things from what I write, but to let words fall where they want to fall. Well, I strive to do this. We are human, you know.

Now there are times I write something and I think it is so-so or I am unsure it will be liked, and it becomes well received, shared, picked up for publication, etc. and I am surprised. I get amazed. Sometimes these surprises come at great times, like when I am low and wondering what will become of me or my work or when I am just doing my everyday ordinary, and I get a word that makes me feel it's paying off and is all worthwhile.

Recently I got some nods of appreciation and one kind soul even called me a "genius." Well, I know I am no genius, but it sure does help your mental meter go up, at least a bit, until you know you must do what you do... because it is yours to do, without praise at the moment you feel you must have it.

We don't always get the appreciation we think we deserve in life. It's why marriages separate, friendships dissolve, and coworkers leave work situations. We have expectations and when they aren't realized we can think the next person or we are flopping. It's just that this is often not true. You can't measure your life, at least on all sides. You can't measure what you mean to someone, or they to you. You can try, and I believe it's good to realize the worth of others, but we truthfully can't.

When my father died, I thought I couldn't love him any more than I loved him. I was wrong. I realize, in the passing of time, we see things differently and sometimes clearer. I love him, fiercely more. I love him more as time passes because I reflect on his life, which was so generous to my own. As the days have passed, I have taken the time to realize what I sometimes took for granted, so I won't repeat that same error in regrettable ways.

Time teaches you things you wished you knew sooner, but it doesn't work that way. It was never supposed to work that way. We are offered this day to make something of it. We have something to give. We will enjoy this day by giving to it and because we care.

## *For Yourself*

SOME OF US have betrayed ourselves. We have doubted and second-guessed ourselves into oblivion; we couldn't even trust our own inner compass, and for those of faith, they lost faith in the goodness of God. When something heavy came down on us, we imploded. We were so disappointed in ourselves and we hated our mistake, our sin, our poor choice, and our failing.

But the opportunities, surely, are not over, unless you want them to be. It is essential to be an ally and dear friend to yourself. Learning to forgive often starts well with you. Giving a break shows up when you don't give up on you.

We often don't have anything to give until we have given to ourselves. It seems so contradictory to forgive or give when you don't feel you deserve it. Pride keeps us from doing that, at least sometimes. We don't want to be seen in a light less than we want to be seen, and honestly, we just need to breathe and understand; it's okay.

We don't always or often hit the bull's-eye but we can still be a part of the joy and process of life. We can get things "right" as best as we know how and free ourselves from self-hatred. It's pronouncing a death sentence without a fair judge. Our eyes may be way more critical than honest or helpful. By coming back to yourself, you will also be doing it for others.

## *The Wisdom Of The Truth*

NOT ONE OF us is exempt here. We all have views and ways of seeing things. We all must guard what is correct, real, and true in our own lives because it goes out to others' lives. I am no genius, but I continue to be baffled why people would love a lie or misinformation over the truth.

You can't solve problems from the point of a lie. You must get to the truth to do that. The truth can be upsetting, but it is liberating, in that you can work from a correct position. Everything you hear is not true. Everything you read is not as it is. Everything you see is not what it appears to be.

Be the difference maker by considering how information travels. Check your facts. Did you examine, by speaking to the person, when someone told you they had done something wrong or so? Did you check out the situation and come to an unbiased assessment of what happened?

Were you there and did you understand the whole story or only get part of the story, and then you base the whole on the part? Do you love the tickling of a lie better than someone's soul or a look at, perhaps, another way the story is or would consider to be?

Don't fill in the blank with others at work, at play, in the home or in the world. Get humble. Get down. Get an understanding before you speak of certainty. It serves dishonesty to place people in categories they do not or should not be, just to have or form an opinion. It's lazy, too.

Truth, often involves some deeper looking into matters. It's often not knee-jerk appearances and conclusions. Put yourself in the place of someone else, and think how you would wish to be seen or believed. Dig for the truth. Give the truth a chance.

## *Honoring Time*

WHEN YOU DON'T know what to do, go slowly. Haste is the disappointer of dreams and peaceful living. We hurry and get hurt or cause hurt. We are hasty and we can't think how to do our best. We rush and we miss what is right before us; what is worthy of our best attention.

It's hard to not be in a hurry. Waiting is difficult. People want immediate resolve for a problem. Youth wants to be older. Twenty-one can seem like an eternity; but for what—to take a drink? How is that your most important event or mission? It will come and things you want to do will come. Enjoy where you are. Don't live your life merely for the "tape" of the finish line. You will be done one day, but what can you do today, that has value and blesses the world—and more specifically, your world?

Love time, without fighting against it. It's a discipline of the mind and heart to do so. It is what you have years and length of days for... to do things better, wiser, and kinder. Never give up, if you have seen the error of your doings, don't let it lead you to despair. Let it lead you to change. You will have stronger days and weaker days. Don't let either of these days move you to pride or inferiority. Be steady. You are not "better" for better days or "worse" for more difficult days. You are human. You are real. You are honest. You are able to make choices in these times; make them!

Make them in peace, without haste, without hurry. Trust them. Trust where they take you. This is your beautiful life. You will not make all of your days from your exact plans because there is always mystery entertained in life, but you are asked to take life and run with it. You are asked to enjoy the freedom you have and the lessons you have learned, and to do something with them. That is being faithful to what you have been given, and trust me; you have been given a lot. It is a wonderful life, all of it and through it.

*Give yourself to love.*
*It will enrich you, inspire you, direct you, create in you, thrill you, and most importantly, it will even outlast you.*

There is always someone to thank and something to be thankful for. I appreciate those who have read my words, commented on them, and who have contributed to the discussion we have shared over the years, both in person and on the Internet. Our lives are a myriad of collective efforts, though we do many things on our own. Each of us plays some part in another's life. We weave similar and different themes of those people on the pages we write. Thank you for everything you have given this life, to me and to those I will never met. It is truly more than you will ever know .

# NOTES

# EPILOGUE

## A Conversation With The Author

### *In Deepest Appreciation*

THANK YOU FOR reading *The Stories We Write: Collections*. It is in direct response to being asked by many... from the many people I meet to those who read my stories in other places.

The stories come from living... from my experiences as a writer, greeting card creator, photographer, and a woman with many passions.

The stories continue because I continue to grow and learn... life over fifty is full, challenging, and at times—surprisingly wonderful. I was once very afraid of this time of life. Married with twin sons, I remain grateful and touched by life, yet my comfort zone existed in all I had done for so long—raise children and care for a family. Now it seems those hard-earned skills served to lead me to another phase in my life.

Throughout the years, people have told me my words convey what they feel, when they were unable to express those emotions, or were told they couldn't or should feel as they did. In fact, a woman in her sixties told me this, years ago, when we were out to lunch. "I've been told not to have certain feelings, but I feel such peace to hear you have similar ones!"

Her words inspired me because we all do have, and are entitled to, the many feelings, which fill our lives. *The Stories We Write* is about us...you and me. It is about feelings and experiences you have and how they are shaped around the stories you write.

I also heard from a woman who read many of the stories from an online magazine, *Hold My Hand*, for which I once wrote. She wrote me saying, "I have gained more insight into my life from your words than from years of counseling." I know it is not because a counselor is unnecessary, because they provide insight and help, but I believe what she was trying to tell me is that she felt 'heard' in these stories and it validated what she felt. This kind of validation often helps us take new steps forward to find and embrace direction and peace in our life.

Our stories are personal, vulnerable and intimate; they are us—beautifully wrapped inside the words we write. We write stories as a way to share how we feel, think, and live. Living, then, is the outward expression of those stories. Everyone has a story; everyone tells a story. Stories are sacred expressions of a life that has been richly lived.

# *A Book Written Just For You!*

THIS BOOK IS for those who want to live, learn, and share their stories. It is for people who want to get to the heart and soul of life. It will not serve you well without the willingness to examine or reflect. Although we do not all have the same need to examine and reflect, the potential results and rewards are the same: a glimpse of how our stories can encourage and inspire not only ourselves in our lives, but the lives of others around us.

People have often told me that I say things that sting at first; a prickle that makes them want to flee or find comfort from what they have read or heard. However, if you stay awhile, you will find yourself stronger and filled significantly with wisdom. This rather philosophical thought comes through my friend and fellow writer, Vicki, and has become the process of how life has worked for me, too.

It is human to feel the need to flee what pierces us, but often, this discomfort is where life's light becomes available and we will do well to pursue it rather than escape.

The stories here were also found in my travels. When on myriad journeys, many people shared their stories with me. You know how natural it is to sit next to someone for hours in an airplane seat. It has long amazed me... the stories given by the person next to me or shared by me as we leaned in to opportunities to give, take, and share our individually earned wisdom.

One man shared a piece of wisdom, after some personal hardship, and it holds its place deep in my heart, to be often reflected upon, "Tell the truth the first time, it's much easier than the second time."

I have had strangers become friends because of kindness, spoken or shared...

One afternoon, on the way to airport, I stopped at a drugstore. The boys and I were getting some Christmas cards before our next flight stop. We finished our purchases and left the building, having ample time to get to the airport.

We were parked on a steep incline, and the kids noticed the tire was flat. I mean like totally no air kind of flat. We had been in the store for barely fifteen minutes. But now the question loomed large in front of me, "How will we get to the airport?" We were not in our home city and there was no one we knew to call. I walked into the store and bravely and loudly asked, "Is there anyone who could help me with a flat tire?"

The words were barely out of my mouth when a man walked over to me and said he would help. It was below freezing outside and darkness was quickly falling. It was a troublesome flat to fix, with rental car supplies being inadequate (someone had taken many tools from the kit).

I now realize I could have called a service, but since we were so near departure time I was so rattled I didn't even think of that. The man just kept at the difficult task at hand, and I told him, "I will be happy to pay you as a gesture for your kindness."

He responded, "I will have none of that! I made the offer because I wanted to help you."

The story ended well; we made it in time for our flight and I subsequently wrote to the local newspaper to tell the story of our angel, who on a agonizingly cold day, offered his help in kindness.

# I Write Because...

I WRITE STORIES to affirm there are amazing people living life, through all that life takes and give.

I write them to tell you those stories often mirror your own—or inspire you to share yours!

I write to share feelings and thoughts, embedding wisdom and messages hidden deep within the stories.

And finally, I write because we must pass on goodness, insight, and wisdom. Life is to share. It is to bless. It is to embrace. It is to tell.

# In Lieu Of A Bio

THERE IS LIFE outside professional work and careers; let me share mine with you. Certain people have suggested I had no job experience because I chose to raise a family. *Au Contraire!* I contest! There can be no better experience than to raise, grow, and release souls to living. Thus, you find my bio does not include a list of professional skills or awards received.

In fact, my most meaningful work was done with little fanfare, but somehow it continues to echo. My children are grown and going forth to make their own mark in life. And now, with the plentiful experience I had as a wife, and touching my husband's life in the golf business, I find other passionate paths. I have rich experiences: I teach and lead children; speak at Women's holiday functions; and play and contribute to the advancement of golf. I continue to **richly live experience**... as I travel to photograph some of the quiet and out of the way places... and share the images with an awaiting world.

Writing was always something I did for me! You can always find me writing or creating; it is what I was born to do, and that which I will bring to the world. I am blessed to use my experience to purposefully mentor to both women in men in formal and informal ways. I have been in the trenches and know they are where real life is found.

In my writing is a voice whose job it is to pass on and tell others, "Yes, where you find yourself is also where you find your opportunity." The message remains, "It's about finding what you are personally responsible for, not complaining about what is wrong. There will be room to complain, but the words must lead you to make things better—even if that includes yourself."

We all have people in our lives that had a hand in molding what we became. My parents were of rich influence. They were often my "go-to" people when I wondered how I would resolve something. Dad left me with these words, "Be good for something." I now counter, "Be good for anything you touch."

This is why I write! I write to tell the story inside of me, which is also breathing in you.

## Life's Journies

I HAD THE distinct privilege to live all over the world as a young girl. My father was a pilot and his work took our family to many interesting, exciting and fun places. Travel, then became the fabric and frame of my life.

There are treasured mementos in my collection: a *cum laude* graduate degree in Finance from Arizona State University, a marriage certificate, birth certificates, evidence of homeschooling twin boys, and high school and college degrees reflecting their success.

As I raised my children, I filled out the corners of my life as I mentored both men and women in formal and informal settings, spoke at Women's holiday gatherings, hosted events and dinner engagements at my home, volunteered with a variety of organizations, and played golf to a 13 handicap.

The time has come to let my growing family go to make their own way and I am discovering the joy and pain as an empty nester. So I write… I paint, I hike and I work among some of life's most amazing people. I am not done yet!

https://www.facebook.com/carolyn.f.mccool

www.facebook.com/FinishWell

sharingawordcdm@gmail.com

# POSTCARDS

I photograph. I write... what better way to put the two together. The postcard section of this book is for quick visual inspiration. A few words, a picture or a little of both often stir the soul. That's my purpose as an author. I can't direct how another person thinks, but I do want to challenge the way you do!

After a very difficult time during my life, I realized how important our thinking is. It's not only a difficult situation or life experience that is hard on us. How we think can make it hard or bearable, just by what we mentally give to the situation. These images are but a sampling here; the actual collection, which you can use to inspire your day, or send to others whom you want to motivate will soon be available on my website.

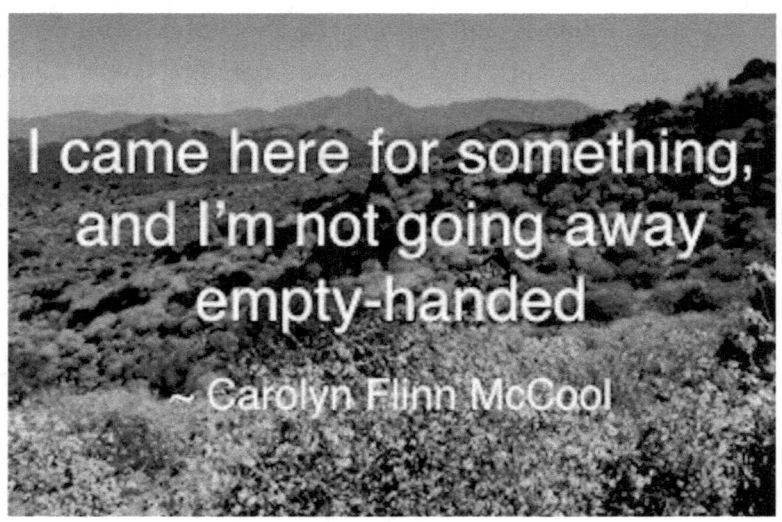

Carolyn Flinn McCool

# READER REVIEWS

If you enjoyed "The Stories We Write" and saw yourself in some of them, you may want to share your reading experience with other potential readers. If you thoroughly enjoyed the book, please leave a review, or tell your friends on Facebook, or Tweet about it. Reviews don't have to be long, complex or eloquent! Just share your spur-of-the-moment reaction; it will help other readers find books they enjoy.

# CURRENT TITLES

*Finish Well*

*Carolyn has a wonderful, introspective look into the human spirit. She believes with all her heart that goodness and mercy are the means to a wonderful, healthy, happy life. The Lord has truly blessed her with this gift. Her words are like presents that one wants to sit and open slowly and savor every word, then tuck them away in one s heart. I have truly been blessed by her work and I know you will be, too. Thank you, Carolyn, for sharing your heart with us.*

~ **Deborah Hancock Tullos**, mother of six, grandmother to 18, married to the love of her life.

*Through this book Carolyn has tapped into the subtle nuances that comprise our hearts and humanity. The notion of 'Finishing Well' is to remind us that our trails through life may not always provide us with a clear path.*

*Sometimes there are obstacles. It is up to us to embrace the challenges and move forward ever mindful of Carolyn's message that we have purpose and we do matter.*

~ **Deborah Andrysiak**, two Master's degrees and longtime friend

*This book takes you on a journey where each reader will find honesty in her remarks about life in general. I believe it will touch those who have struggled, like she has, with the issues in life and make one see, there will be light in the darkness, eventually. Her story just makes you feel you are not alone and we are all normal!*

~ **Nancy Codi,** fifteen times Saucon Valley golf champion, painter, and outdoors enthusiast

Carolyn Flinn McCool

## The UnCan Man: Feeding You From The College Years And Beyond

We often think of opening a can when we need something to eat. College students or young people on their own may be inclined to do the same, but there are options. Change the way you see food. The *UnCan Man* helps a man eat well, without the need for a can. Inside this book you will discover what kind of *UnCan Man* you can be with instructions and recipes to fuel your life!

# NOTES

Carolyn Flinn McCool